The dVerse Anthology

Voices of Contemporary World Poetry

Edited by Frank Watson

Plum White
Press

Also by Frank Watson

One Hundred Leaves: a new annotated translation of the Hyakunin Isshu, Editor and Translator

Fragments: poetry, ancient & modern, Editor

To learn more about Frank Watson:

Poetry Blog: **www.followtheblueflute.com**

Twitter: **@FollowBlueFlute**

Email: **followingtheblueflute@gmail.com**

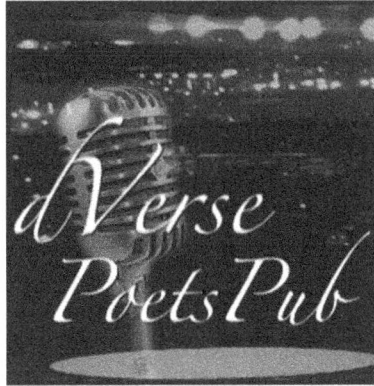

dVerse Poets Pub is an online watering hole for poets from around the world, designed to inspire and provide a stage for their voices. Each week there are opportunities to share poetry and opinions. At its heart, dVerse is an ever-growing community of word artists. Stop by dversepoets.com and see; you may never leave.

Table of Contents

Credits

"The Missing" previously appeared in the poetry anthology *Velvet Avalanche*. Reprinted with the permission of Joy Donnell.

"Quilt" previously appeared in *Notes for the Translators: from 142 New Zealand and Australian poets*, ed. Christopher (Kit) Kelen. Macao, ASM, 2013. Reprinted with the permission of Rosemary Nissen-Wade.

"valentine's day" previously appeared in *Modern Haiku,* 44.1 (2013). Reprinted with the permission of Ben Moeller-Gaa.

"from the hammock" previously appeared in *Frogpond: 35.3 (2012).* Reprinted with the permission of Ben Moeller-Gaa.

"autumn wind" previously appeared in *The Heron's Nest*, XIV:4 (2012). Reprinted with the permission of Ben Moeller-Gaa.

"opening the blinds" previously appeared in *A Hundred Gourds*: 1:3 (2012). Reprinted with the permission of Ben Moeller-Gaa.

"morning fog" previously appeared in *A Hundred Gourds*: 1:2 (2012). Reprinted with the permission of Ben Moeller-Gaa.

"melting ice" previously appeared in *Haiku Harvest*, 6:1 (2006). Reprinted with the permission of Polona Oblak.

"torn cobweb" previously appeared in *Haiku Harvest*, 6:1 (2006). Reprinted with the permission of Polona Oblak.

"rain-filled river" previously appeared in *Mu,* II (2011). Reprinted with the permission of Polona Oblak.

"flurries of willow fluff" previously appeared in *tinywords*, 11.2 (2011). Reprinted with the permission of Polona Oblak.

"becoming cold" previously appeared in *Notes from the Gean*, 3:3 (2011). Reprinted with the permission of Polona Oblak.

"Subway to the Center of the Earth" previously appeared in *Bora*, #2. Reprinted with the permission of Frank Watson.

The dVerse Anthology

Voices of Contemporary World Poetry

Lyrical Seducer or The Poet Cad

Suzy Rigg

Undress me with your words
Seduce me with your pen
Excite me with your stanza
And you will be my man

Impress me with your verses
Deflowering every word
Use skills so subtle and words so rare
And you will be my man

Digress not from your mission
To pursue me with your prose
Paint the air with peacock rhymes
And you will be my man

Parade your love of words
Toss out your finest style
Demand I listen fully wrapt
And you will be my man

Colour me with language
Arouse me with your voice
Pull me in with tender tricks
And I will have no choice.

Believed

Katherine Bischoping

Saw you barefoot in my dream, stirring
Brown lentils for a new sick pup, setting
A wooden spoon down on scratched-up
Turquoise melamine. Your tongue
Stuck in that place you'd broke a tooth.
That pup, all baffled in a teatowel.
Folk remedy, you said, as I leaned
My forehead into your shoulderblade,
And I believed.

melting ice
the letter
i hesitate to answer

Polona Oblak

rain-filled river
the things
you kept from me

Polona Oblak

torn cobweb
he tells me
he'll never marry

Polona Oblak

A Pretty Face

R.H. Mustard

A pretty face
still beckons me home,
soft voice calling
my name alone.

A simple touch
on my heart still,
a forgotten memory
years cannot kill.

Each waking hour
your hand's on mine,
living now
outside of time.

In the waiting grove
down by the sea,
I find the place
you saved for me.

This is my heart

Yiota Karioti

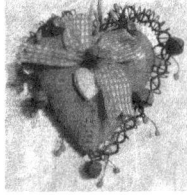

This is my heart
Most days it beats
Measuring time in sun rays
And old forgotten love songs
When darkness comes
My heart listens to the rain
Dripping like a half broken hourglass
That misses seconds and minutes
Marking Absence with Longing
This is my heart
For every fallen leaf
For every hidden thorn
For every tear that flows
For all the goodbyes and hellos
It blossoms forth
In the middle of your soul
And i cannot stop it
Singing a winter night's song
Red and gold
And i cannot stop it
Soft like angel's wings
Fragile like many precious secret things
Just a whisper around you

A halo that dims
The luminescent dust of broken dreams
Your eternal twin reflection
On the secret shore
Of Love
Always together
Never apart
This,
Is
My
Heart...

Wulfstan

Glenn Buttkus

We were hours deep into
southern Louisiana one spring,
marveling at the darkness at noon,
as the sun fled, hearing a tornado warning
barking from the car radio
and for a brief blink everything
                            was
                        deathly
                      still
                    just
                before
                  it
              rained
              so
          hard
          we had to pull over
to the side of the highway
followed
by the bellicose bellowing
of thunder
as we witnessed
the terrible beauty
of God's veins
turning electric
when crackling shards
of spider web lightning
stabbed jagged holes in the sky,
and the air was full of wolf god howling,

and we both knew that
there was a towering wind demon
nearby, swirling up farm trucks,
bath tubs, and lives;

a mega-monster
with scythes and talons
and flashing white eyes
dealing in a dozen kinds of death
and daring us to tread
within its alley.

When We Were Three

Marvin Welborn

Come now.
Come and go with me.
Together we'll walk
    round the red maple trees.

Down past the block,
we'll walk and we'll talk –
Old Henry with you,
and me will be three.

We can make believe
as we used to be –
three old amigos,
back when we were three.

Oh! those sights and the sounds,
just the way that they were
when we made our rounds,
when our souls would bestir.

So come now. Please come.
Take a walk with me.
And we will pretend
like it used to be.

We'll stop on our journey,
    periodically;
where you'll smell the same flowers,
    occasionally.
A rabbit, a squirrel,
    or a cat, you may see.
What brave little souls
on your leashes with me.

Robust, bravado,
when we three would be
on our own little journey –
our own odyssey.

So, come now. Come!
Come walk with me.
Where we will pretend
that it's still just us three.

And Henry, now off-leash,
from both you and me,
dancing and prancing,
so merrily free.

Let us pretend
as when we were three –
Old Henry with you,
and me would be three.

The Unknown Frontier

ninotaziz

we seek a place where perfection of prose beckons. on white parched paper the ink flows freely. prettily. each and every sentence makes perfect sense, only to you. a thought takes you places high up, real low, over the bend and beyond

> somewhere beyond
> that layer of thought
> words

we seek the inner plateau where the higher conscience beckons. on the road of life, thoughts flow freely. deeply. each and every idea makes perfect sense, only to you. profound discoveries take you places high up, real low, over the bend and beyond

> somewhere around
> the bend of the river
> stream of consciousness

we seek a book where small stories beckon. on a parchment, legends flow freely. enchantment. each and every folkloric magi makes perfect sense, only to you. an adventure takes you places high up, real low, over the bend and beyond

> somewhere
> captured in the moment
> small stones

we seek refuge where religion beckons. on wings of faith, hope flows freely. divinely. each and every revelation makes perfect sense, only to you. compassion takes you places high up, real low, over the bend and beyond

> somewhere high up
> mountains of hope
> revelations

we seek enlightenment where poetry beckons. on each leaf, grey stone, pebbled road, words flow freely. uplifting. each and every poem makes perfect sense, only to you. a beautiful verse takes you places high up, real low, over the bend and beyond

somewhere deep
below oceans and gut feelings
inspiration

Wild Geese

Tony Maude

Spring begins with wild geese;
wave after chevron wave
of feathered trumpets
sounding encouragement,
straining forward,
dragging the reluctant sun
to lands too long deprived
of light and warmth.

a cup of tea
she runs her finger
around the pacific rim

Sondra J. Byrnes

The Five Languages of Love

Vivienne Blake

Chat-up lines
sweet talk
pillow talk
I do
baby talk

or

Chat-up lines
sweet talk
pillow talk
silence
goodbye

or

Table talk
tea in bed
tender care
telepathy
no need to talk

valentine's day
the warmth of old love letters
in the fire

Ben Moeller-Gaa

Drawn Towards the Blue

Geetaa Suri

octave of emotions,

crumbled me n my creations...

it was a mystical touch,

was a brash single impression,

shortcut to tranquility seems wiser,

but was out of the blue,

 to disappear in the oblivion......

uneasy to hold....

Intense instincts of

Me myself n I knocked the nerves,

the vision of the soul is cleared,

wanna draw towards the ocean blue ...

a blue clematis
speaks
for the sky

Sondra J. Byrnes

Quantum Leaps

Victoria Slotto

I dreamt
I flew among the stars,
  skirted between planets,
  cracked open doors
  to distant worlds.

        I dreamt
        I plunged into the deep,
          touched ocean floors,
          sifted through sand
          for hidden treasure.

I dreamt
I tunneled to earth's core
  midst roiling, writhing magma,
  set free the Watchers waiting
  for redemption.

        I woke
        I drifted toward the sun
          and grasped a ray
          to turn back time
          into my dreams.

Flight of Fancy

Mary Kling

I was walking through my dream
when I met you walking through your dream;
together we found a dream to follow
until both of us disappeared
into the dream of someone else
who dreamed you a handsome prince
and me a golden-haired maiden.
And together we rode white horses
by the light of the silvery moon
and fell in love under the stars
until the dreamer became jealous
and wanted you for herself.
So in her dream I lost you,
for she dreamed me without you.
and I never met you in dreams again
though I looked and looked;
but I keep hoping you will find me.

Through an Open Door

Joan Barrett Roberts

I
dream
of
you
regardless
of
what
you
say
your new one word storyline
reveals a secret
hidden among the roses
red bleeding from night thorns
your wishes shattered
where rivers flow against the shores
I dream of you
regardless of what you say
it's only a rainy day
a quiet time in October . . .
aloft in my dreams
where deadly day-fires grow
your pulse lingers in the wind
will I follow . . .
through the open door
over looked moments unspent
among our restless souls
my true love knows no limits
unless you are free
to be
I
dream
of
you
regardless
of
what
you
say

In my dreams
I build a castle
Where the shadows dance

夢の中
築いた城に
影踊る

Frank Watson

morning fog
the sober glow
of streetlights

Ben Moeller-Gaa

Early Morning Coffee with Mary Oliver

Victoria Slotto

In early morning
dappled light,
I sip poetry.

Nature
breathes freshness
in the flawless new day.

The shadow of a hawk
skims dry-grass gold
of a nearby hill,
swoops down.
Blackbirds nag.
Wrens and finches punctuate
from pendulous
cherry tree branches.
Flashes of orange
meet orange
to copulate.
Red hot pokers
seduce orioles.

Ample branches
of the ash
conduct the choir.

Applause!

from the mind
of the closet . .
a cricket's voice

Sandi Pray

an old woman
is she the new old
or the old old?

Sondra J. Byrnes

The Grand Ol' Hat

Margaret Bednar

The
Good
Ol'
Edwardian Days
When swirling skirts gracefully
Swept the floor, ankles carefully hidden.
Puffed up like a proud pigeon and resembled
An instrument measuring time.
Oh, how to show
Individuality? Dare
We suggest such a
Thing? A prim and
Proper young
Lady
Must wear her hat squarely
Upon her head; no silly feather, please!
But, if one had a desire for a bit of frivolity, well a trip
To the hat maker might just do the trick. A feather added and tilted
To one   side, a splendid ornate hat to promenade. A   multitude
Of other   frivolous items could grace the crown: A poppy,   a plume,
How   about a large cabbage rose? A bit overwhelming?   Well,
That was   the very idea! To have fun, live a little, after all,   it was
Just   a hat. The only thing exposed   was
Hair!   Sometimes splurged, and added a   bird?
Well,   Not a whole bird,   nor
Even   a   whole
Wing.   For   many
Years,   Twenty   in fact,
The   Audabon Society   fought
To outlaw such animal cruelty!
Even hat pins were subject to the law!
Why, they could only extend so far - dangerous
Weapons they. Known for poking, scraping and stabbing!
Regulations on how far they could protrude without hat-pin
Protectors. Some were banned from public transportation, in fact.
So, no whole birds, but how about bunches of cherries, blackberries
Or ribbon rosettes? Hats made to whirl, flow and dip; some swathed in
Tulle. Some glorious hats mysteriously rested upon the hair, thanks to
The secret of "wadded" hair saved from thy very own brush to make the
Grand pompadour! Possibly a bit of mystery might be desired; was that
Even allowed? It could be arranged with a bit of cobweb trim hanging
Over the face. Social gatherings were not complete without one's hat,
In fact it was part of proper etiquette. Quite disgraceful to be seen
Without! Even the little widow could not step out... all in black, of
Course. No feather for that would be too gay, but the veil was ok.
Oh yes, the good Ol' Edwardian Days! Most likely styles to never
Be seen again. Glimpsed by some of us still alive as we watched
Our grandmothers step out. Those wonderfully grand ladies who knew
How to dress in style, held on to their "vogue" until the very end. White
Gloves, snap purse dangling at the elbow, and perhaps, the hats a
Bit smaller, but there none-the-less. Ornate glasses framed many of
Their smiling faces, pearls circling their necks. Still buttoned up with
Proper skirt line maintained, although a few inches shorter. How "modern"
They must have felt. So here's a nod to the grand ladies of old, who wore
Those hats with such style and grace. How were they able to carry off
Such hats as these? Looking at the photos, their eyes might offer a clue.
The   Women's
Suffra   gette's
Atti   tude?
In Courage   And Honor.

My Great Aunt, Jennie Beckington, 1905

My Grandmother, Marguerite Hutchins Beckington, born 1892

owl song—
my bath full of shadow
and starlight

Sandi Pray

sleepless . .
the path from my bed
to the Pleiades

Sandi Pray

Dream

Victoria Slotto

Last night I dreamt of
feathers and shape-shifting.
Today a wren perches on a naked branch
outside my window.
By afternoon
the tree is in full bloom.

snow falls

i n t o

countless little

(wet)

kisses

Frank Watson

What it is & a game of checkers

Brian Miller

i had this epiphany, sitting
on the couch:

> never let words
> get in the way
> of what you are trying
> to say

& wrote it down, in my notebook.
right next to another:

> i am
> nothing
> without proof
> of life

& even a thought in the margin
on a title, 'My middle name is Timothy
not Thomas' ~ a little personal truth
emphasizing the spiritual slant
of 'i am'

but feared it might overpower the zen
in it, and doubt scares many when you start
asking for proof --- it sucks

not many think
about what they're leaving behind, until late
in life --- i let a kid in class flip through my book
of rhymes & out of all of them,
he picked it out

'you wrote this?'

'yeah, don't know what to do with it yet.'

'what's it mean?'

'i dunno yet, you tell me.'

& he couldn't yet, but wrote it down
to process later, like i did when i got it
thinking it needed more, some fancy words,
slant rhymes or meter to make it meatier
or palpitate its heart, but in the end it's
just words, an add on, a pretty bow,
a fancy cup for a man dying of thirst
when all he asked for is water

making it more about me
than him anyway ~ and we
have enough of that.

The Butterfly Effect

vb holmes

Time is. Has been. Will be.
If we could change the past
Would the future still be
The child of the present?
Which present?

Earth, The Dress

Brian Carlin

I don't see some fastidious god
tirelessly tacking
handsewn stars,
to twinkle in layers
of black taffeta'd night,
eternally perfecting her look.
More some teenage prom queen
whose universe,
in the big bang of a wardrobe search,
lays strewn:
a kaleidoscope of worlds.
And somewhere,
small and blue,
Earth, the dress she was looking for.

On the Corner of a Teenage Flame

Laurie Kolp

I stand on the corner
of goodbye,
my mouth a broken branch
dangling in the bitter wind.

I watch you sprinkle sorrow
in a field of broken dreams,
then turn your back and leave
me languishing

on the corner
of a teenage flame.

you and me
like dark and light
like crawling lines on the back of your palm,
my snow white collar bone.

Lily Wang

zenzizenzizenic

Saiqa Aftab

Your page sir : my liege : is in contrarily most vexed, pressed rice for dressed blessings tests some next flex messing wrecks, battling sexes : sick exes : I am lost in your vortex : your cortex : your core text : every word a stalking whore fest, every perplexing angle is a hex manifested in correct : missed context : contentious : content is us : content us : is dichotomous. Failed bullets bubbling from holes out your neck. Distressed. Eject. EJECT-EJECT! All consuming depths, tumbling decks like a house of cards bleeding broken into a cascade of open surgery hearts.

You forget me with a capital M, when you should be leaving the rest of them...

Crestfallen, remembering caresses undressing innocent skin, my I you digest : die in jest : like I'm under arrest : staring at naked spirits within. You read me my rights yet I stay on your left, melting, bereft of heart strings, you mark my words as you follow through, debating. Serenades, stilling. I'm whispering, inside my soul to keep me, believing, I'm every thing I want to be, I'll progress my achieving, I refuse to be something, that I'm simply not breathing, you can't mould me into a being you conceive by stealing false teachings. Son of a... preaching man, your nature's deceiving, a soliloquy delineating memories denied as untrue, cookie fortune crumbles into mumbling prince of thieves I'd die for you.

Set free from delivering a future I thought was me and...

You protect me, Lord only knows why. All your voices are blind, fumbling in the dark with nothing to find. I was right here, the whole time. Sway me. Language of courting and courtesy. I gave you mercy. Fierce kisses. Curtseys. Were you worthy? Lamenting love, chalice of fallacy challenges your alleged tragedies: I'm not dumb. A means to an end devoted to incentive led outcomes, sensitive as molten lead then molesting originals...

Suggestive subliminals, my heavenly is...

Holding me at arm's length, disclosing close proximities, you're limited, brimming with disingenuities. Am I making sense? You. A malicious genius emanating incongruities, desperate disparity despairs my discontinuity, a spare part, this par pares a con parlaying I was the only one, I guess shallow clarity is better than none, the less, I dismantle your obscurities and wish you be gone. Propelling security selling insecurities all along, your pretending maturity, false sense of purity, locking on to a point blank canvas first...

Scourge of the earth fussing for second desserts...

It hurts. A lot is too little: a brittle fate is too much to take. Sedated. I wake. Ninety nine days too late : a plaster on your wound switching back to hate : too stubborn to wait, choosing imperfections, an empty crate filled with bottles overflowing space. Stitching heavens, losing direction, my affection disaffected, mingle and mangle into a painted face unredeemed.

...and in a dream nothing in words is anything it seems...

You : my : side : now : said Adam to Eve. I want you : beyond the biblical : Made her Lucifer leave. Reckless : fair : weathered. Her she being deceived : a tale as old as time muttered the beast. Playing baitly : daily : slaying maybe. Troubled : paradise : bereaved. Paired dice scattering treble tongues swiftly deceased. Killed him sweetly : clipped : wings : ceased, to flutter beneath : wind sings stinging : billowing willows demeaned : cyclical tail feathers : sick little tale peddlers : ruffled fables released...

I'm on : a see : saw
if you : feel me
believe

I Drank Poetry

Christena Williams

Bartender
Pour me some more
Let me stumble through the back door
Let the police
Smell the poignant aroma of rhythm and blues
Collide with my Genius creative expression
Handcuff me for resisting being silent
Check my breath for the bubbles of a drunken poet
Spitting up words and rhymes
Expressively with profanity
Charge me with intoxication
Verbal sensation
Before the judge
I plead guilty
Poetic confinement recommended
On the walls I write art
Painting out the graffiti of the prisoner's thoughts
And colouring with poetic expressions

Bartender
Pour me some more
Until my cup overflows
I just can't get enough
Let this liquor become embedded in my arteries and lungs
Let it be in my very DNA
Let it flow through my blood and veins
Through my heart and mind
Let it be hypnosis for my dreams
I drank poetry and it tasted delicious.

she feels great
maybe she should get
a second opinion

Sondra J. Byrnes

Closed

Mark Windham

I stare at the closed door.

I do not expect her to come
through it--
we are beyond dramatic
entrances and reconciliations--

but it is interesting, to see
life defined by which side
of the door you are on,
and who has closed it.

She paused there,
before she left,
waiting for me to speak,

I lied, and said "I understand."

whenever i think 'Bear Parade' i think of large, hairy gay men marching down the street

dom schwab

there will always be
moonlight and
lovers and
kissing

but these
cannot
apply to us

Naughty Wind

Kelvin S.M.

Listening to William Carlos Williams

Brian Carlin

The needle clambering
the shellac road
has sharpened its
contact point enough,
whilst garnering fluff,
to mimic your
cut-glass tones clip-clopping
through
crackles,
hisses,
strangled bubblewrap
and one deep scratch
which repeats
at seventy-eight beats
per old minute,
clicking over something
about a "white desire, empty"
and is either a flower
or a hand,
or nothing;
and the thump,
like the trip
of a boot on a stoop,
has me hearing
the dust blow forward
from the paint-flaked porch
of 1940s America.

Quiet Grief

Mary Grace Guevara

across the sea
tinged with mottled moss and weeds

you called like a black raven
trilling high on apple tree

sated with sweet corn,
coarsely piercing the calm of day

my hands gathered pearls,
moist silk, to fall on your cheeks

seeking your eyes in misty green,
to lay like a fish on your crest

body wet, wedged deep in water,
warmed by southern wind

but the fire-lit sky devoured all
into clay, and suckled dry by sun

you see a cold, unmoved stone,
but i tremble with each word

flowing from your lips, each ripple tide
of quiet grief and unlit verses

floats softly into my ears,
and i dream of you again

lost in the sea

Alone

Kelvin S.M.

Of this morning sun and peaches

Mary Grace Guevara

the sea tide followed you this morning,
clinging to your hair, dripping of corn and sun
bursting at the seams with rounded seeds

the shell case broke open, replete with seeds,
and for the first time, my tongue tasted morning,
naked, lush pulp, succulent fruit under bittersweet sun

nothing prepared me for you, flaming the sun
sky with words drizzling like apple knotted seeds,
staining my room forever silky bold, unlike any mornings

this morning, sun dawned, tinged red of pomegranate seeds

Once Upon a Time II

Addie P. Abbott

I write this Letter,
At an age where I'm supposed to know better.
Where I'm supposed to be clever.
Where I'm supposed to be smart.
Intelligence dictates that for me to enjoy the gift of the future
My past is where I should start.
And I should ignore the present...
For now I am flowered with a Love that's been rooted in thorns.
Smiles no longer warm my soul,
But scorch my feet through a stride of hypocrisy,
And a laughter that pierces my ears like horns...
I rose to be a Liar.
Forgetting to stand up for what I believe in.
Meaning Morals and Values were no longer intriguing.
Faith, Was just not worth believing.
Yet I swore I was always doing right.
Success never left, she just succeeded in deceiving...
Miss Direction became Miss Leading.
Engaging me in a polygamy that centered on me cheating...
That told me my Love should be shared,
So why from the ladies of the world my secret I was keeping...?
I never knew I needed to be shielding...

I write this letter,
at an age where I didn't know better.
I didn't comprehend weather.
Didn't realize that I was subject to the reign...
Predicating my sentence,
But not changing my story.
For the novelty of hypocrisy meant there was never sincerity in me saying
"I'm Sorry"
Never good wishes in a wave,
Never comradery in an embrace.
For compassion had long drifted,
Chivalry had long been martyred.
And the blood of Love had been tie-dyed into religion.
Where for Respect, Sacrilege had been bartered...
Feelings became Colours.
Colours distinguished races.
Races raised racists.
Men of Love became sadists.
Spontaneity raised Rapists.
Premature deaths became the latest...

The basis:
Where envy breathed life into a generation,
And heart-felt comments were poisoned with a hatred painted by the greatest...

I write this letter,
To the Age where I hope things are better.
Where things are clearer.
Where Society remembers not how to smile with a heart as Cold as a Sheffield December...
Because I remember...
All a little too well.
And I pray you don't drown in the search to quench your thirst,
For remedies to cleanse your heart and remove the hurt...
Ash to Ash
Dust to Dirt.
Understand Love,
Understand Worth,
For As I Write this letter,
I aim to show you to be earnest;
Targeting the good in people.
To take Shots to raise the bar!
Not just crowd it,
Crown it.
And the irony is I'm writing to myself...
For the ink of My Past leaks...
Onto the pages of my Future...
But not affecting My Present...
For the Gift that you are, My Son,
Is one treasure that I will never regret.
For who you are now,
Is who I was...
Once Upon a Time.

Eastern Mountain

Anonymous Chinese poem, translated by Frank Watson

I left for Eastern Mountain,
And long I did not return.
Now I come back from the east,
Beshrouded in drizzling rain.

In the east they said we could return,
My heart in western sorrow.
They made us beautiful clothing
And whipped us no longer.
Silkworms curled about
Along the mulberry field;
They rested alone
Beneath our carriage floor.

I left for Eastern Mountain,
And long I did not return.
Now I come back from the east,
Beshrouded in drizzling rain.

I carried betel seeds
And brought them to my house;
A spider lives there now
And spins her web by the door.
Our village fields are open wide,
And deer shine bright on their nightly walks;
I must not fear,
Yet this I hold in my heart.

I left for Eastern Mountain,
And long I did not return.
Now I come back from the east,
Beshrouded in drizzling rain.

The crane cries on a hill,
My wife sighs at home,
The drizzle clears the sky,
And I journey, to arrive at home;
There are bitter plants and wood
For fire from chestnut trees.
How long we couldn't meet—
Alas! For three years now.

I left for Eastern Mountain,
And long I did not return.
Now I come back from the east,
Beshrouded in drizzling rain.

How they fly to heaven,
Their feathers shining bright;
When I married my wife,
She came on a speckled horse.
Her mother tied her bridal veil,
And then the ceremony was held.
That new life was so joyful,
But what happened to the life I had?

Crossing the Desert

Kelvin S.M.

Gypsies

Priyanka Dey

Sky
Mine
And yours
An onlooker
Gypsies;
In commotion.
One moves forward
Another, backwards
A step or two
Motioned always.
I stray; I wander
Meandering awhile
Borders beliefs and horizons
—All alike.

my semicolon

Saiqa Aftab

Verging on two paths.
One of water. One of rocks.
My heart is vast.
You'll not ask,

and I can't find,
words hide, terms shy,
conditions undecided,

black and white resign to define,
an entity, my ball of energy,
my serenity, identity, free radical:

you stand before me: logical, practical, magical:
you're my aura all the time,
each thought an antidote for my poison mind,

lettered mimes, reasons rhyme,
your raptured spirit glitters mine,

sensitive, every tiny pore is craving to be felt, every sediment in my delta
melts, just a slip of a finger or a lick in a breadth against the smooth nape
of your neck, a slick caress, it's a nude guess, sultry kisses,

painted into golden scented shreds, illuminating shadows cast by your
sunset, breaking moulds, beads tumble into tempting folds, attempted
hold, stubbled brushes against reflexed collarbones, you close your eyes
and see stars fall,

we see saw, and this with just a lip kiss on this bit of skin form, your air's
warm, sticky, sweet, mingling in the heat, a generated still from
anticipating a deeper real, our surreal,

hands feel shoulder blades, souls made from hazel stays, skies scrape as
curves shade, we lay swayed, spines surrender to stroking craves,
gripping waists, sober tastes, seconds surpassing jaded ways, no more
time wastes, better late than...

dawn quenches yawning days, clawing, glowing veins to chase, paving
mazes phasing bodyscapes, our arteries shake, flesh trembles, fears
escape, tipping fingers inside dipped vertebrae, clicking, collating, scaling
intensity,

inking calligraphy with dignity...

he sits, blessed by the grace of ember quivers, remembering blisses, succinct glimpses, fractured and full each sliver delivers, silver shivers like diamonds glisten, delicious grins, listening, to me dreaming, his demeanour considers,

hearting senses, half-whispers, breathless, melting cordoned fences, psychological defences... my sensai... shun all... his arms call: I delve, he envelops my crumbling fall into a sensual disarray,

I stumble on words and he kisses me for... play, pray, for it to be this way in all ways, always... I take him, strengthening embraces, it's amazing, liberating, lacing faces with blizzard flakes,

temperature raises, beating skips paces, praising names, holy places, encased in races stating no stasis with this status, our basis set, lost in check mate, wrapped in his swirling oasis, placated, propitiated, conciliated...

reaching into scriptures written in trust, dancing equations balancing us.

Resting

Kelvin S.M.

Letters from Provincetown

for Juno

Frances Donovan

I. Becoming

The beautiful woman in the mirror
takes her clothes off:
                    she becomes me
with the ankles thick in the wool socks
she becomes me
                    I am missing you
the distance between moon and water,
the distance between you and me pulling
like the tide, difficult to say without
becoming clunky ankles without—

The beautiful women all around me,
they writhed and shouted.
They tipped back their bottles.
They leaned on their pool cues.
One to the other, each one different,
each one shining, luminous
like the stones at the edge of the surf,
beautiful when wet, within their element,
unremarkable when dry, outside of it.

II. The beautiful women, the angry sea

I met a woman from Plymouth
dark hair, fair skin, Portuguese,
child of sailors
            child of slavers
                        child of fishermen
She carried herself like a tightly packed pistol.
She spoke an English I barely understood,
chopping her vowels,
            clipping her consonants
                        with a laugh at the end
I danced with her
we wove a dark silk cord between us
she bit me on the shoulder
                    she made me shiver
                        she disappeared

I took a woman from Kenya
to the beach.
She was smooth and dark and full of curves.
It was raining.
            In the dark,
we stepped off a sand dune
and fell eight feet through emptiness.
I could hear the ocean beneath us,
               beating his angry drums.
He was hungry.
We clambered in the sand,
                  it crumbled beneath us.
I don't think we can do this, she said,
and I shouted *We have to*!
I was angry at the waves beneath us
and I was angry at the darkness
and I was angry at the rain falling gently on our faces
and I shouted and dug
                  into the crumbling cliff.
I put my hands on the miracle of her ass
and pushed her up.
I pulled us both over the lip.
Sand was in our clothes,
it was in our mouths.

I kissed her. She tasted like liquor.
I drove her home.
She asked me in, but I declined.

III. Missing you

Missing you has taken over my life,
turned my mind into a battleground.
I will not think of you, I will not.
Pulling up from sleep's highway,
I had a respite.
            There was a view, which I've forgotten.
There was the ocean, and scrubby pines
and a beautiful woman with dark, curly hair.
I remember touching her skin, its smoothness,
soft, hairless, luminous, like the stones
wet at the edge of the ocean.

But then I remembered you
and the pull began again.
Missing you here is like missing you at home
but with the smell of the sea
                        and light all around me.

IV. Whale watching

The boat is full of Germans.
They speak a language of consonants.
The boat lulls me,
        bumping against the tires on the docks.
The sun is warm on my face.
Soon we will push off into the deep
and see huge mammals that swim in the sea.

Someone at the wheel knows these waters,
can read the charts of them,
has sailed them before.
I am glad to be on the boat with them.

This boat is full of Germans kissing,
Americans kissing, man to woman,
woman to man, blatant and unconscious,
knowing and unknowing,
even here, at the tip of the continent,
                        with their baby carriages,
                                with their dollars.
If you were here, I would want to kiss you
and I would be one of them. If you were a woman,
I would bury my face in your breasts.
I would put my hands inside you
and you would feel like the ocean in August,
you would taste like the sea.
Instead, you dive into me. I push against you,
your body hard,
                angular,
                        covered with hair.
I love what's inside of it, the watercolors
inside the twisted contours
of a painting by Egon Schiele.
After whale watching,
                I am too tired to miss you.

V. Becoming

On the beach, I lie under a dune and shiver,
thinking of you, how it would be
better with you here, how we'd roll in the sand
and pick the wet stones from the edge of the water

and I remember the story you told me,
on your back beneath me
                              with tears in your eyes,
about the woman who loved you
and your child inside her

You weren't ready, I'd said
on my knees above you.
You couldn't have had that happiness
even if she'd stayed.

This is akin to my wish
for you here beside me now

A little sigh,
She looks at me—
The black-feathered bird
On a dark branch of spring,
Elegant and desperate.

Lily Wang

the scent of her bosom

Val Termane

the scent of her bosom
draws the swallows
into the night
and I smell spring
between her thighs

Footprints

Ali Brown

Ghostly footprints
In the snow;
Paths and lives
Criss-crossing and
Frozen
For a moment
In time

a blood drop

Val Termane

a blood drop
fallen from the ceiling
drew a wingless angel on your face
and i smiled in derision
but after
devouring your little feet
reddish like wild poppies
the chest started to burn
bringing my heart down to ashes

Graffiti

Ali Brown

The flock of pigeons takes off
Leaving their silhouettes
On the red brick wall.

Nocturne

Tiara Winter-Schorr

The last half of the night is mine to keep.
I collect these hours like unstrung beads.
When you leave, I do not give in to sleep,
but allow the darkness to offer counsel when I am in need.
Sounds of seduction and desperation are carried on the air,
its scent slick with garbage, piss, Newports, sweat
and the promise of rain. When you leave, I no longer care.
On the nightstand, an empty journal brims with uncharted regret.
Your first true love is music but I too am music,
surviving each night in mutilated harmony.
The hours are tumbling towards morning, bluesy and slow,
and across the way church bells are an alarm to me.

If 3am is the hour of the soul, then I live in the hours past redemption
with broken notes and a ravenous heart.

the songs we played/MisSing

Claudia Schoenfeld

tobacco crumbs
from hand-rolled cigarettes in
the corners of my mouth, i

couldn't play yet, sang along,

brushing carpet fibres
with two fingers one way,
then the other, as we turn

complicated codes into songs,
wrap 'em in thin light,
moleculed emotions (those,

you can't grab), we tie carefully
with barrier tape to chords
in DSharp (mostly) (black&/Yell
ow/bLack)— see— this is
what i mean, the gaps
get smaller

with each song & puff,
exHaled, (your stepmom
never wore a bra, smoked
Javaanse Jongens, dutch brand—
on the fridge, to do lists
for the week)

you loop the capo
'round her 6-stringed neck,

i turn the page,

no need
to really talk much

Vi(r)gilant

Karin Gustafson

My rearing more classical
than equine,
I never understood why
you shouldn't look a gift horse
in the mouth.

Especially if you wanted
to scope out
hiding Greeks.

I imagined peering down the maned
gullet, muzzle cocked, as I stood upon
a chair in High School English, faces
in the dark chest cavity torchlit,
alarmed.

Illustration by Karin Gustafson

Sans Eyes

Karin Gustafson

Time
sands eyes, blunts
retinae, but as distinctions dim,
I tell myself, a unique
camouflage
is limned; so I notice, in my peer,
how the tufts of white-tailed deer
mock milkweed, puffed pendula
over thickets of fall-browned
fur; my blur
is almost proud of this newfound likeness
till I mistake upon the ground more pods, soaked,
for a chewed hoofed foreleg,
and now, on the slippery
of this steep hill,
as the translucence of evening thickens, I stop,
transfixed by the loom of each branched stick, barred
by the barbed unravel
of somewhere fence, all
nearly swallowed whole
like poison
disguised in draught, razor blades
spiking a sweet, till just the second
before we meet,
some shadow
shapes sharpness.

And what am I to do?
Stuck, as night falls,
but use hands
to look ahead, and screw up
what gaze I have
as if sand could be molded
into something
that would actually outlast
this tide.

Today

Ali Brown

I could write about the bread I made
This morning
Or the cinnamon sugar
Mixed with maple syrup on the
Pancakes, or
Not being able to afford to travel to
London;
I tried to write about
The bluetits and dogs and
Snow that was falling gently
In the park;
But maybe I could write about
Homemade pizzas instead, and then
Sitting by the fire with rum & coke &
Leonard Cohen;
But somehow I can't find the words
For any of this, because today
My head is full of Loss
But I can't even write about that...
So I'll just sit for a while and
Be mindful, and with gratitude
I know that
This will
Pass...

An occasional table, dreaming

Katherine Bischoping

An overture, an orange peel,
The ocean's opalescent eels.
The onerous drains, auteurial games.
The au courant says au revoir when au début
It thought of you –
Now ordinary, then so strange.

The open windows overlook
An oleander's opaque scent,
The aubergines loll on the vine,
A two-hand nocturne skips a beat.
Occasionally, a table stands,
An oval whorl tipped to its feet.
A heap of books slips slideshod off
And Dover Beach falls to the oak –
Opa! Olé! Oohs and ah,
Love, let us be true.

The table sways, tiptoes a ways,
Again it sits, again to sleep.

Alarm Calls

Ali Brown

The blackbird's call
Rushes through the open window
And in the distance
A siren screams.

A Night In The Rain

Umesh Rao N

As the earth is savoring rain's refreshing kisses
He starts recollecting his treasured blisses
Sitting beside an open window
He takes a stroll in memory's meadow.

Horns of vehicles play the background score
As he reaches to his mind's core
Quenched are all his senses
As he tears down all his prejudiced fences

His long, uncut hair flies in the cool breeze
As he makes these moments to freeze
The trees glimmer with glistening leaves
Rain pouring through cloud's sieves

These clouds decorate the canvas of the sky
Making the whole scene a treat to the eye
Pondering about who is its painter?
He bows in awe and gratitude, to the almighty creator.

A Meeting of Straying Minds (Valentine)

Karin Gustafson

Love is knowing (sort of)
that when I, the vegetarian for many years,
grow even more decrepit, forgetful, blind,
you, who have never truly understood beans,
will not feed me meat.

It's a pact that I've repeatedly extracted—
"you promise," I say, nearly tearful, and you reply,
blushingly, *yes, no, of course not*, so I'm pretty clear
that even as you too grow old, you will not
slop me into a chair with your extra chop
at my chin—

But what worries suddenly
is me:
that, after decades of non-carnivorous cravings,
I will slaver, in my senility, for
your sirloin.

At first, you will saw the cuts with resistance,
your elbow blocking my claw, but,
as I whimper, you just might,
in some trumped-up trompe mind's l'oeil,
excuse the bloody bits as for my good,
a poor woman's Procrit,
and, careful to whittle away all gristle,
spoon some down my craw.

On the one hand, this a problem in our love—that you give in to me—
and on the other hand, this is a problem in our love—
that you never do as I ask—
and on the third and fourth hands—because thankfully
we have them (clasped), this is also our great wonder—
that you, who try always for the meet and
right, no matter, will be there with me, even
demented,
promoting your sometimes skewed
but always sweetened sense
of my true needs, even if they involve
my grazing from your plate
(something you absolutely hate
in anyone else).

Though I wonder now whether I shouldn't get the words
"do not feed meat" tattooed—
only they would have to letter my forehead—(I can't imagine,
as we recede, you reading below my sleeve)—
and I worry that, with such a phrase emblazoned, people
might feel that they also should keep me from knives—

And there can be so very many lives
in a single life—take the one you lent me when
my old had emptied—
that it is perhaps better to keep vows off
of one's brow, even those about meeting someone more
than half-way, the way you meet
me, though that line admittedly shifts sometimes,
while somehow our hearts stay always
in the exact right place.

Red as . . .

Katherine Bischoping

Red as wagons
As Nana's box that Squirrel came in
As fat wax candles and first nail polish
As stripes on ribbons in typing class
As filing folders, print on sugar packets, Persephone's
    three-seed lunch and Diet Coke
As in walks an office fantasy . . .
Red as the east, eight hundred million little books and all
    the signs that night in Chinatown
As blood, as an apple, a Gala, Campari, a slapped cheek,
    the veins of a Jonathan and recklessness

As his eyes at sunrise

And his eyes, years later, from the blood-thinners
As a tea found only in Canada
As pity.

Waterfall

Apryl Gonzales

Cascades of liquid resonance,
Washing over solidarity.
Erosion of fury,
Stripping away
The prudential resolve
Of assurance

Pressing
Again, and again,
Into the softness
Of wanting Earth
In surrender

Union of substance
Fluidity unsubstantial
The pouring of fleshly inclinations
From the soul to the ground
And they find course there

Fleeting moments, fluent touches
Seared into the limestone of the mind
In absence they exist
Impermeably

Necessary touches
Powerfully brief
Takes away with it
Marrow of soul and sand

Forever altered
By the pounding
Composition decomposing
While men lie watching
The water falling

The Raindrop

Jeff Newport

the raindrop falls
from the tip of the
magnolia leaf bearing

the reflected world
falls and breaks into a
thousand tiny worlds

Frozen world

Andre Pace

interest did not
lead him
characterized
my work
"student should be trained to know
 the antiques so well that they can be drawn from memory"
splendid
anatomy
spinning was the artist
sister
"fancy"

if a man sees the world in a way that is deeply his own he cannot help
registering that difference in everything he does and says

When It Has To Be Right

Chris Lawrence

ethereal light shimmy
protruded through pale drapes,
my aches as moving from bed
to floor,
mouth dry tongue stuck
and contorted,
folded into some origami,
a dream shelved
some fragments hinted
at a vividness by spangling
in my conscious,
today would be different,
all ideas of what would be
had silted and taken ferment
for me to sift and filter
in an abstract way,
and collect my thoughts and speak
ignore at the time the cacophony
of voices that had alternate advice,
she would be exquisite as usual,
the dragon of my yearning
would have to wait,
until that moment of coda

Innocence Unbound

Mary Kling

Innocence merged with defiance, reliance,
she stands her found ground unbound,
breaks rules like dishes whenever she wishes,
and her frilly dress swishes so womanish.
Her mother anguishes as she watches
the kittenish joy of young Helen of Troy
who struts her stuff without compliance,
leaves all around in spellbound silence.

In Winter's Sights

Jennifer Wagner

she placed snowshoes on the mountain,
a shine to the lips of heaven

in a musical crunching of white
with peek-a-boo pine cones and twigs

it was in moments like this she felt it,
breathed it

when douglas firs and lodgepole pines
held a shimmering of frost

and a barn owl's low hoot
gave her a sense of mulled cider

when the fire is just right
and so is the world

Airborne Mechanics

Chris Lawrence

i took her to the roof
to find the sky
that she left behind
last year,
unable to identify
position of the sun
or what color the
clouds were,
i had to let go of
her hand,
so that she could reach
then float onto a backdrop
of blue,
feel and process the sky,
acknowledge it was all
wrong
and that the moment we had,
had then
was different,
my own hand
could not find
her ankle to withdraw her,
bring her down,
she raised higher
and i called,
but those soft shelled ears
included my voice with the
natural sounds,
and i became absorbed,
where was she going,
i was on the edge
teetering brink of infinite
moments,
would i fall
or find flight with her,
too afraid to discover
held back i watched
the darkening sky,
a sun paling to moon
wait till tomorrow

Tepid thoughts

Maria Wellman

Tepid thoughts lazily floated through the air never to be acknowledged by
actions.
They are expelled genius wasted on inactive dreamers
leaving fruition a far off fantasy.
The stores of these lost ideas and musings, If they could only be honored
by unearthing
their captured secrets.
Maybe someday the stories of these lost ideas and musings will be told.

That thin girl with a box of doughnuts

Richard Archer

That thin girl with a box of doughnuts
I wonder if
Sugar glaze
Has ever passed her lips.
Or saturated fat
Has ever threatened her hips.

That thin girl with a box of doughnuts
Is it true
That vanilla cream
To you is a Body Shop shampoo.
And blueberry cream
Is just the colour of your front room.

She Lives on Second Avenue

R.E. Warner

she lives on second avenue
among newsstands, barreling traffic (sometimes
still), whistling for taxi cabs, buying barter
ing, trading and a one,ooo hollering shaking
cheering giving taking easymove figures with
somewhere else to go.   she listens from above

cinnamon nutmeg hand, dotted hereandthere, rests
and soothes a smooth stomach (dotted hereandthere)
caressing her belly her hand lightly rests swirled
above a din and hum flows downtown honks and
screeches winter blue and cold gray outside
huddle the window and cuddles scarf hat glove
covered folk, mad and happy with
somewhere else to go.

not to slide easily from her sunlit filtered
burrow (warm with incense sweetness) unadorned
curiosity flowers grow up from large brown eyes
to bloom when they press the ceiling.   she sighs
a sound above the hurleyechoboomswish and clang
      and a dog barks

Mademoiselle of church bells laughs at white noise
she hears the joke and punch line stowed like gold
underground buried there on second avenue.

No turning back

Andrew Kreider

Someone in this sea of black and blue,
of downturned eyes, has a tattoo
on her shoulder blade – a butterfly
perhaps; better yet, a devil's eye
that no one but her lover knows,
a secret that she never shows.

Someone in this modest fashion show
is wearing orange, brazen just below
her neckline, bursting with desire
not so much to shock as just to let the fire
within her have its head at last – finally
to be the blazing torch that she was born to be.

Someone in this close and holy space
is terrified, yet ready to depart this place
once and for all. Tonight,
after the benediction, no fight
no grand pronouncements, no bitter end.
Just a kiss, a plain embrace for every friend
and then no turning back – her fierce reward for
loosening the tight-tied strings her mother wore.

I.

J.S. Petri, translated by J.S. Petri and Frank Watson

As a cold wind
that's wet with tears,
so autumn peers
through empty rooms.

A wooden ferry creeps
to shore along the weir,
where shadows seep.

The boat is strained
with fruit and grain,
cut and fallen, drifting
to a long, shifting death

as the sun sinks deep
into red and weighs
the commandment of sleep.

Original German

Herbst geht durch den Raum
wie ein kalter Wind.
Die Weite der Leere.
Eine hölzerne Fähre
geht
zum Ufer, wo die Schatten sind
durch sickernde Wehre.

Liegt Obst und Korn im Boot,
gefallen und geschnitten, treibt
in einen langen Tod
wie Sonne sinkt
in eine rote Schwere
und Schlaf ist Gebot.

II.

J.S. Petri, translated by J.S. Petri and Frank Watson

Tired lawn,
wet grass,
sky of slate,
days of glass—

a walk with broken shoes
to unknown doors—
but which to choose?

Who knows where
it begins. You're snared
in a heavy spell,
remaining to dwell,
but the room has nothing there.

Original German

Die müde Wiese,
das nasse Gras.
Der Himmel aus Schiefer,
die Tage aus Glas.

Mit gebrochenen Schuhen gehen
in ein fremdes Nebenan.
Wer weiß wo
fängt es an.
Gleiten in ein Schwer
und seinen Bann.
Zu bleiben, wo man kann
und die Zimmer sind leer.

III.

J.S. Petri, translated by J.S. Petri and Frank Watson

In the wind, the leaves
go down the stairs
and flies swirl and grieve
without relief, to their death.

There is an ancient tree
with peeling bark;
its roots lift the heavy mud
and sink back into earth.

Cold silence crawls
through stoves and halls,
calling out for the woods.

Original German

Geht Laub die Stiege im Wind,
taumelt Fliege, wo letzte Stunden sind
und sucht
nach Raum und Halt.
Am alten Baum
schält sich die Rinde
und Wurzel liegt und hebt
die schwere Erde.
Schweigen wird kalt,
kriecht
in Öfen und Herde
und ruft nach dem Wald.

IV.

J.S. Petri, translated by J.S. Petri and Frank Watson

A sound—a sea song

Infinity descends
so deep and dark
and every house extends
as in a line

tired as berries
ripe as wine

Original German

Ein Klang. Gesang der Meere.
Das All
geht tief hinab
da geradeaus. Und jedes Haus
ragt hinein,
müd wie eine Beere
und reif wie Wein.

the shape of absence

Kelly Letky

is always drawn through tears
on the tails of falling stars

and just like the pleiades
cannot be seen
if you stare directly

but only exists
in the corner of your eye
or someone else's

just a habit whisper
phantom ghost
heard only at midnight

and in the after echo
of the twelve stroke
dissonant chime

the silhouette
of negative space
is deafening

dark winter's day—
the silence of a sunset
without a sparrow

Sandi Pray

the rise and fall of my chest
quietly I breathe
a sparrow sings

gennepher

leaves
fall
I let go

gennepher

With apologies to a great man

Andrew Kreider

It's no use. No matter how hard I try
I just can't see why people like this book.
I mean, I know that Shel was a great man
and all, but as far as I'm concerned,
The Giving Tree's an abomination.

Whenever my grandma read me this book,
the room would crackle with self-righteous pain.
Her sad eyes would well up, reminding me
of what she had sacrificed for my sake,
all the while hinting this was my fate, too.

My heart would bounce between guilt and loathing:
I didn't know which one I despised more,
the tree that wouldn't stand up for herself
(and please note that the tree is female)
or the man who kept coming back for more.

Talk about a complete lack of boundaries –
go ahead and chop me down, that's OK –
If that tree had just had a therapist,
maybe she wouldn't have let herself be
run over by a narcissistic child.

My friends, it is high time we took a stand.
Next time anyone suggests banning books
in schools, this one should go top of the list.
You want to have good morals in our kids?
Then teach them that true love sometimes says NO.

A Weary Passenger

Margaret Bednar

The moment he walks through the door, I know

his arousal isn't always sexual
more often partners with animosity,

a cumulus cloud gathering force
with every perceived injustice.

Uninhibited alcohol fuels this jet,
instability hovers, careens into
violence, cumulonimbus like.

I dare not look toward his thunder
know it will dissipate quickly,
beg forgiveness of me,
a weary passenger.

I try and soar above, ride out
another night, another flight.
Hope my eyes will witness
morning's slivered moon,
gentle light, proof I survived.

Amid This Lonesome Bliss

Rhonda L. Brockmeyer

Replete am I, amid this lonesome bliss,
Encoiled within my broken, fleshly shell.
I am sealed within, by a writer's kiss.

Unfurled Orchidaceae Kafkaesque.
Sepals veined with secret, all to dispel.
Replete am I, amid this lonesome bliss.

Screaming from within, fearing the abyss.
Spinning colours like fine-webbed carousel.
I am sealed within, by a writer's kiss.

Sunlight glanced my path, to not go amiss,
Alighting dark holes in which others fell.
Replete am I, amid this lonesome bliss.

I endure another swing of solstice,
Darkness bleeds to Light's vigoroso swell...
I am sealed within, by a writer's kiss.

I have been granted nothing, but for this:
Release of mind so the tide does not quell.
Replete am I, amid this lonesome bliss...
For, I am sealed within, by a writer's kiss.

Love at Versailles

Andrew Kreider

Of course it was, since we were but
seeing ourselves in the other, busy
reflecting and being reflected. A glorious

palace in France, where I was the king
and you Antoinette, and we gave them all
cake and white lace, while the congregation sang.

Soon enough came night to undress us both,
and we were strangers after all, running
through crowds as the tumbrils rolled.

For what is love, at last, but chasing
down cobbled streets, an irrational hope,
while every passing face thinks you mad.

the best scene from The Omen is when the nanny kills herself

dom schwab

i used to think the best scene from The Omen
was when that guy got his head sliced off
by a flying pane of glass

but that was because i was young
and adolescent and liked violence
when i saw the movie

the real "best scene" in The Omen
is also the scene that contains
the best line:

"It's all for you."

that's what the nanny of the antichrist shouts on his
fifth birthday just before she jumps from the rooftop
with a rope around her neck

and her swinging body crashes into a first-story
window and everyone screams in horror
except for the antichrist

the antichrist does not scream or look horrified
the antichrist looks at the nanny's corpse
with calm indifference

and likewise, the poems and the stories that i write:
"It's all for you." but i don't know who you are and
i fear you'd react with calm indifference too

Better than I am

Mary Grace Guevara

Red lights at the bar flicker smoky flame
I order wine & cheese, savoring flame

Slow music brings strangers to dance sweet &
tangled kisses – but I drift, waning flame

Moonlight gleams on my ordinary face
Anxieties mothballing, snaring flame

Heat soaks my hair into knotted brown ropes,
I pen words – coarsely pale as dying flames

I might look better if you dim down lights
To candle tap, softer flowering flame

My dreams bring me wading out to the sea
Weaving a storm with fingers – snapping flames

You gaze at me with awe, breathless, inflamed –
Here I am, better than I am – beautiful flame

Orange Sneakers

Dianne Turner

The connection of the here and now
blurs into abstract visions of orange sneakers
together with other crazy shoes, scattered over a bedroom floor.

Lost in the disarray of future pursuits,
intermixing with torn dirty t-shirts, hair gel,
bourbon cans and unfinished studies.
Longing to pound the floorboards or city streets
with the gusto of youth.

The energy of those fluoro sneakers grabbed me,
that's how it is in the city,
a sudden attack of memory
when a stop sign gives you pause to think about orange sneakers
and their purpose.

Can you remember, as you stand there with your stop sign?
As if you're God or something like it,
speaking
to me
in that
tone.

For less than a minute my mind wandered
to those fluoro orange sneakers
and okay
I wasn't paying attention
when you turned to slow,
slow is what got us here.
You know it, I know it, feeling that strange sense of one shoe missing.

Out there, tonight
a pair of fluoro orange sneakers
with other crazy shoes
will sneak past stop signs?

Orange sneakers know this world is fast,
seconds are vital,
standout and stride to the next illusion.
Connecting dots.

Here we are losing seconds
you losing patience.
Glaring at each other
all because we failed to see the importance
of orange sneakers.

The Deep, Dark and Lovely Wood

Rhonda L. Brockmeyer

There... in the Deep, Dark and Lovely Wood,
I'd stop and stay, if I could.
Allow you to pull me into your kiss
Wrap me in the sweet seduction of your unknown bliss.
Find me with your scarred and tender soul,
Caress my mind, fill me until I am full.
Until I'm weak at the sensitive backs of my knees,
Until I'm yours, to do with as you please.
Pull me into the mist upon the ground.
Lose myself in you, until I am found.
Healing my wounds with feather-soft balm.
Laying inside your embrace of reassuring calm.
O, to lay there in your warm hold,
Sheltered from this Northern cold.
Let me fall asleep, curled into your breath...
Let me sleep there, deep as death.
To awaken to find your eyes holding me safe and secure,
A sleep of love, untainted and pure.
To wake, and hear what is upon your mind,
A fear, a joy, a sadness, a past rewind...

An echo calls me from my dream where I slept

And with sadness, my silver willow-green eyes have wept

There... in the Deep, Dark and Lovely Wood...
I'd stop and stay, O, how I would... If only... If only... If only... I could.

Skeletal Remnants of Spring

Rhonda L. Brockmeyer

Mirage

R.H. Mustard

The desert heat
numbs the world,
slowing me down,
tricking my memory.
At the airport,
planes avoid touching,
are somehow
still moving.
On my phone,
arrivals and messages
blur. No one can say
when your flight
might be landing,
whether I should
even be waiting,
in this terminal
where we all come
to practice departures,
or if you
are still searching,
approaching from afar,
an illusion,
shimmering up
from nothing,
like before.

A dire dream

Sreeja Harikrishnan

A blue jeans hangs from the string, water dripping,
A blue sky shines, deep; no birds flock but sit winking;
A bird perched on the string, another on the tree,
Whole courtyard has birds perched, at every corner.

A blue jeans hangs from the string, water dripping.
A room, doors jammed; window opens a world, breathing,
A gadget, a genie; a screen that brings conflicting spree
Freedom, freedom; all lions, and no other species near!

A blue jeans hangs from the string, water dripping,
Dripping into old scribbles, portraits, fables – fading,
They leave scars; abstracts form and meanings blur.
The birds – not one rises into a flock – sit in corner.

A blue jeans hangs from the string, water dripping,
Endless pastures, all lions, no other in sight, straining
Eyes, ferocious fights, and a life cycle blocked, a mere
Joke, freedom laughs and responsibility mourns, here!

The doors scream to be opened, a dire dream, shakes.

approaching thunder . .
the turquoise tang
of a faraway sea

Sandi Pray

between cedars—
a redbird follows
the white wind

Sandi Pray

snow as white as breeze through a swan's dream

Sandi Pray

Solo

R.H. Mustard

The empty bowl
is left out for me
the night before,
its knife and spoon
so clean, reflecting
the best intentions.
The cereal box
is standing tall,
fruit chilling
in the darkness,
all awaiting
my attention.
You know I'll slowly
eat alone, wash each
dish and wipe it dry,
I'll make
this room comply,
so you will see
how I'm still here,
hoping you
might come by.

mac

Ewan Lawrie

i guess it is at that
a name for all the no goods
i ever met standing cool
on the corners
pitch and tossing nickels and dimes
blue collar loser takes all

it could be a cop though
it s the uniform nightstick blow
right across the shoulder blade
in the alleys
ride the trolley buster and dont
come back now that s all

and tough guys spit it out
round a lit smoke to wise guys
who read a lousy movie script
on the sidewalk
speak Sicilian words and phrases
you don t believe at all

you guessed it right im mac

Wend

Rhonda L. Brockmeyer

I sat in the lone, frightened chill of dark,
Eyes, covered in deep rusted enclosure.
I had never felt light or steaming warmth,
Just shivering fear in cold exposure.

His hands had felt along, blindly in the dark,
Hesitantly, fearing what they'd reveal.
I felt his warm hands upon my cold flesh,
They felt the scars that had begun to peel.

He grabbed me tight, about my broken wrist,
Pulled me upward from the dank, frozen ground.
His eyes were sweetly deep and amber kissed,
Looked with pity at the mess he had found.

They wandered about my wrecked, tattered soul,
His heart spilled forth with golden, fractured light.
He held me close as breath, traced my silent pain,
He saw the evidence of my lost fight.

His tears fell, dripping compassion freely
They washed my bloody and dirt-sullied face.
My breath grew shallow, I felt death approach...
He begged me to not leave him in this place.

He trembled to see me live, see me breathe,
But I was so weak, my mind turned to black.
He grabbed me up, carried me in his hold,
Down the worst length of a perilous track.

I felt his hot breath against my smooth neck,
Heavy, hurried under my broken weight,
He carried me along, tripping, falling,
Enduring this tiresome, exhausted fate.

Every time I whispered weakly, "Please,
It's okay, leave me, put me down to die."
He just held me tighter, sweeter, clinging,
I cried silently, could not fathom why.

Through all the dangerous paths that wound on,
He carried my broken soul, held me dear;
In the dark, the storm, the thunderous night.
I could feel, in his body, creeping fear.

Finally, we emerged, a bright clearing
Filled with blazing light, warm and lemon sweet,
He collapsed us to the green ground, breathless...
I noticed only his tired, bleeding feet.

Then he wrapped me deep in his arms and placed,
Kisses gently upon my cheeks and hair.
His breath still ragged, trembled, pained and short,
He looked at me with eyes of tender care.

Relieved, my body unclaimed by death's grasp,
He closed his eyes, head laid upon my breast.
I watched him, my eyes danced with deepest love,
Felt my heart swell, bursting inside my chest.

I watched, his sleeping eyes flutter with fear,
Raged by nightmares and terrors, foes unseen,
He awoke within my protective arms,
"Shhh, my love, it was just a tortured dream."

I whispered gentle, a dragonfly breath,
Against his ear, skin grazing my lips,
Soothed his worry, felt his pulse slowly calm
Traced his painful scars with my fingertips.

"I knew," he whispered, with his amber eyes,
"You were worth the journey to hell and back,
That you were worth every jagged step.
You were worth braving a frightening track...

I knew if I left you, laid you down there,
Inside that dark place of terror, you'd die.
At that moment I knew I needed you,
Though I must admit, I did not know why.

But here I am, entwined deeply with you
Against my skin, feeling alive with love...
It seems, your heart and soul were made for mine,
Gifted to me from the vast, blue above."

I looked intently into his sweet eyes
Deep and ancient they were, as amber stone...
"It is true, from the moment I saw you,
I knew you were my one, only, true home."

Brisbane Heatwave

Dianne Turner

Weeds embellish the side of the rail bridge
strands wilting over red brick
bleeding into the road beneath
where yawning cars wait in line

nearby the river laps the edges
winding a necklace embrace
of promised relief
for this flustered peak hour city

the city dips its toes in the cool water
with an ah... almost audible to those who
cannot speak in cars mustered against
the invisible fence of red light heat

on the top of an apartment building
an oasis glows in Christmas light
surreal palm trees beckoning with the breeze
that blows across the top
of a summer cocoon

wisteria drops the last of its weary blooms
the flame tree pales to pink
under the evening sky
life is one long sigh
waiting for the lights to turn green

Demystification

Glenn Buttkus

"Poetry, whose material is language, is perhaps the most human of the arts, the one in which the end product remains closest to the thought that inspired it."
—Hannah Arendt

American haiku has
the feel of leather chaps
in every line.

A prophet wandering
in only concrete canyons will
not be heard.

The homeless man
sleeping in my doorway has
found his sanctuary.

The dragon's breath
can sear flesh, or it
could be sweet.

A samurai sword,
although it is usually decorative,
always cuts bone.

Frost on my
redwood deck railing shines like
King Solomon's jewels.

My old tomcat,
Keezie Moto, loves to sleep
near my head.

The Fuji FinePix
S4500 captures my wondrous perceptions
with effortless grace.

All stone bridges
bear the weight without the
assistance of steel.

Washington State sports
a ring of fire within
four active volcanos.

There is beauty
found wherever patina leaves its
fabulous rusty footprints.

We are surrounded
by castle ruins as testament
to history's folly.

I dream of
Scotland as if I had
lived there once.

I cherish poetry
the way misers covet their
piles of gold.

Jack Collum is
a pragmatic poet worshipping words
rather than syllables.

Gift

R.H. Mustard

The steel claw,
with its shiny arms,
has dug me deep
into eternity.
The metal vault,
with its polished dome,
contains my restless sleep.
When you slip away,
remember how well I fit
beneath the dazzling tree,
how wrapped up
I am each year,
with expectancy.

first light—
an egret searches the edge
of darkness

Sandi Pray

not quite dawn—
the milky breath of
a newborn calf

Sandi Pray

Synoptic Puzzle

Dianne Turner

Oswald's sliding down the coast
like a big cyclonic snail
rain trail globs
flood the coast
while my husband solves puzzles
with falling blocks
that never fit together
the way you'd expect

all sides being equal it's not so strange
that Oswald should visit and stay awhile
the rain dancers expected him
and smile

they called him with wishes kissed into the air
and his big burly blob sits on the front porch
leaving huge puddles on parched earth
that rush down to the rivers
overflowing with the tides

He's not completely unwelcome
and there's not much choice
on the weather menu of extremes
dry toasted landscapes
bushfire charcoaled scenes
remnants of summer turn into soup of the day

the blocks fit snugly
into the puzzle
that's not exactly right

And as what's left of Oswald's tail
whips the air around us
my husband gets a high score
and we wait for the deluge
expected to be another record breaker
all things being equal

If you were here with me now

Martin Shone

Balancing upon a dash of dream
is where I sit thinking of you

flowing as only a bubble can
my thoughts bounce and shimmer

so impossibly thin is this dash
I tremble as I balance
as I sit
thinking
of you
and only you

If you were here with me now
I would tremble still
as a tree quivers
in the ache of wind's kiss

of you
and only you
I sit
and think
of you
and only you

If you were here with me now
I would become silent
...as the stars
where there is an aching
...solitude
so far
so far
yet
their light
touches
to reach
the eyes that see
and the hearts that know
that in the stars
there is love

only you

If you were here with me now
I would smile
as the first fall of snow
kisses the earth
I would smile
as the earth sighs
beneath its blanket
I would smile
as the second fall of snow
waits for the crunch of life's touch
I would smile
as life's touch
is your touch
I would smile

and kiss you

-

...but you're not

Past Masters

John Anstie

If I had ever taken note at school,
those moments often shunned by one poor fool,
of literature, philosophy and poems
that offered us the sustenance of tomes.

Be gowned, the masters strenuously plead
that sonnets and soliloquy we read
to dress our minds and feed our souls with love
of words that speak a language from above
our mundane daily toil; speak of the day
when I am moved with eloquence to say
I understand... "Oh, now he understands!"

And when I feel my heart in her soft hands
I move to paint her love with words I see,
embedded in my mind; sweet mystery.

(A Clarean Sonnet)

Elephant Highway

Suzy Rigg

Unbalanced carts spilled sun ripe fruit
on the dust strewn road
splitting colours, splashing seed
to meet the market dawn.

Spindly children tried to run
alongside heavy traps
some were strong and long of limb
and barely caught their breath.

Bicycles, too, took their own road
and weaved their wheels about
the death they cheated,
although in jest, made
villagers shout out loud.

The noise grew low
for something strong
had taken up this path,
a silver grey bull elephant
was on this very route!

Without a sound
the track was cleared
of children, wheels and fruit,
whilst Mister Majestic walked
~ in no par-tic-u-lar hurry ~

Without a backward glance.

The King of Uig Bay

Tony Maude

With his back towards the dunes, he waits alone,
while moon and stars traverse Lewisian skies
and pass unseen before his staring eyes;
the king of Uig Bay, seated on his throne.

He never sees the white of coral sand,
is heedless of the ocean's rise and fall;
as, unmoved by the corncrake's rasping call,
eternally he stares towards the land.

Unperturbed by pounding waves and gales
which howl in winter's never-ending night,
steadfast through the returning of the light,
limitless, his patience will never fail
for he knows, beneath the fleeting summer sun,
that one day soon his Uig queen will come.

Summer Memories of Mordialloc

Dianne Turner

Some see the beach like a cool gem
glazing it over in pastel tones
sand softens to cream, dimpled so gently
with ultramarine footprints
over the dunes
subdued colours lying behind heat haze and salt spray
beauty captured like a garden in a bottle
yet no matter how beautiful the impression
the beach in summer for me is like a visual shot of tequila
colour that hits you all at once
splattered with drops of sunlight dazzling upon blue
lightening to turquoise where the waves lazily flop
leaving white lattice webs to weave and disappear
into the jaune brilliant and Vincent yellow shores
voluptuous clouds slowly saunter across cobalt blue skies
sometimes bursting like kids screaming "I see it, I see it"
that welcoming strip of blue at the end of city streets
with lollipop umbrellas, dotted over the sand
the smell of vinyl as we sat in the back of that old Holden station wagon
where the warm north wind carried the aroma of fish and chips
through the wound down windows

Rest

Lori McClure

Summer rays send us running
for a softer side of earth.
Balance,
bounty,
beauty trickles
through trails of
burnt orange and yellow.
Remember and forget
the business of sun's
refining, melting
down
into sloppy puddles.

Oh, messy change.

In-between
blazing and frozen
we all
fall
down
around sweet licks of a cool kiss laced with
wind swept crumbs
between
sweet sticky-fingered
love
left for two on a blanket
(by a fire).

Stars held up with sticks found in the rustle of a wood
wait to welcome
even the weariest of dreamers
once again.

New Year's Day

Marvin Welborn

Black Carrion birds
   encircle the sky,
in search for the dying or dead.

A lone little squirrel
   scampers right by –
A whole 'nother world lies ahead.

Last year's leaves
   still cling to the vine,
they rustle and rattle in wind.

An old man clings to the end of a line,
the dog, to the end, a best friend.

New Year comes on
   past the last, having gone,
and the moment goes on to the end.

New Year's Day, as someone will say,
is the same way New Year's always been.

Again, and again;
   and again.

Inside the Diorama

Dianne Turner

I woke to the sounds
of a gently gurgling
brook
while I rubbed my eyes
an egret sidled
alongside me
and froze
like a statue
watching

I dared not move
his stare
intense
captured the moment
and I wondered
was he
confused

suddenly
his head shot forward
he pulled back
with a fish
that he swallowed
and then
continued
on his way

somewhere above me
came a chuckle
I sheltered my eyes
from the bright morning sun
a smiling face
of a Chinese man
looked down upon me
from the rock
on which he sat fishing
"he only wants the little fish...
not great big whale"

"ha, ha, yes," I said
rising to my feet
"I wonder ... could you tell me where I am?"
"Ah you're right where you're supposed to be
at this moment in time."

a strange quiet
was apparent behind
the whisper of water
and it was as if
I could see for miles
yet everything seemed
so close
the man saw I was puzzled

"You're very lucky,
a trip for yourself
here
to every place
both near and far
that so many never see
a precious moment
lost in time
that quiet space
between"

and the egret, stationary
plotted his
next course

A Certain Slant of Light

Victoria Slotto

There's a certain slant of light—
the way the sun slices through half-opened blinds,
of a late afternoon in autumn.
A single star and fireflies
on a new-moon night.

There's the sound of cricket calls,
a desperation to be heard,
the creak of wood-on-wood,
the texture of the rocking chair,
thick white paint, over paint that tells
the tale of those who came before.

There's the taste of tears,
so many drops of loss,
the flow of pain down rounded cheeks,
my mother's soothing touch.
That's when I learnt, too soon
curled up upon her lap,
of death. There's that.

Note: Titled after the first line of an Emily Dickinson poem

Land of eucalypts

Roslyn Ross

In secret, slivered slip of leaf
the frame is put in place,
a languishing of eucalypt;
as perfumed, drifting grace.
The myrtle from the southern land
is born in fire and death,
and drapes the days in waiting
until it burns again.
With serpentine releasing,
its skin is shaken free,
revealing flesh fair beautiful
as bark surrounds the tree.
The moon shines on its purity,
caresses milky trunks,
as phoenix-like she rises
on watered, ancient roots.
Like demons born in torment,
they raise igniting arms,
as if to cry for mercy
when nature calls them home.

La frutta*
(reading the paper placemat at Colombo's)

Andrew Kreider

Start at the heel of the boot,
at the sumptuously-named Lecce,
and run your finger around the graceful
toe, beaded with Sicilian heat.

Move slowly upwards, pausing at the knee
to genuflect at the Holy City, then on
to gaze in awe at the high-swept sinews
of the landscape leading up to Assisi.

Come around the thigh, taking time to
taste the savors of Bologna, Parma, Genoa,
circling over and round the graceful
inland swell of the northern provinces

and down, down again to glide
upon the glistening canals of
Venice, whispering softly as the
red wine disappears like a sunset.

[*Italian for "The fruit"]

Old Men at Sixty

Marvin Welborn

Old men at sixty,
forget more each year;
but once when much younger,
a world, a frontier,
old men at sixty
were, too, cavalier.
Now old men at sixty
they forget why they're here.

Old friends get harder
to remember, revere,
as memory grows flinty,
the past, unclear,
old men at sixty
forego all their fear.
For old men at sixty,
soon learn why they're here.

When old men were twenty,
the world was their sphere.
As young men, had plenty
of future, career.
But now, passing sixty,
a white-washed veneer,
old men at sixty
too soon are not here.
Old men at sixty
soon learn why we're here.

Angel Voices

Charles David Miller

Needing to be seen, I find my face
in the mirror and shave away the edge.
The lunatics on the street know me.
They whisper my secret name and splutter
profane histories that riff jagged chords
from out-of-tune wire. They beckon me to join
on bended knees and supplicate the God in you
at subway landings, our long greasy hair
draped over nugatory faces, neither male nor female,
our fingers hung like rotted fruit at the end
of dead tree limbs that beseech heaven
for pity, compassion, a stranger's stray dollar.

He hid under the covers and spoke
to the mother ship all night. At dawn,
he killed the dog and set the piano on fire.
The Others had come to take him home.
He spent months in the observation ward
and left with a pocket full
of antipsychotics and Gillespie
itching his finger tips with no way out.

They see one of their own in me, those lost
and despised. Like them, my past is one
long short-circuit of happiness. Their pain came
unasked, but mine played as perverse desire
to warm my self in its own burning ruins.
Criminally flawed, I'd bury my bone of deceit
in your chest and dig it out to chew on.
There's no crime I could not commit,
given the right circumstances.

When the meds milked his soul near empty,
the stars conjoined to tear him in two,
and his need to celebrate their harmony
so fated his blood, he quit eating the poison.
Lightning lost itself in the keys on the piano
and the chords of Gillespie spoke in angel voices
from the mother ship and mingled with mating songs
and drug deals in the dead end bar.
Dawn light on the Sangre de Christos ran red.

In the kingdom of the lost and insane,
the realm of saint and sinner, being seen
is not being seen, and not being seen
reveals our nothingness. Truth dies with you
in the grave and burns like an ember slowly
losing its glow. Only then do angel voices
open the gates of heaven or hell.

In the mirror, I shave away one more angle
to reveal yet another part of me that I might be or not.

Southern Hospitality

Jeff Newport

and yet, not so many years
ago, we hung our black
brothers and sisters
from our leafy gallows
as we posed, grinning white
faces topped with jaunty
hats. Smoking, squatting
on fatty haunches,
or leaning against
the strange fruit-
bearing tree as if sharing
a neighborly moment
in the white clover yard
of the white narrow church.

The First Breath

Laurie Kolp

It's the first breath,
when candlelight stirs a dormant hunger
longing to escape the busy day
and whispers fill the air
with night's approaching din
as we unwind, a peaceful solitude.

The breath that passes
through the sky in streams of silk
oranges, reds and purples spread throughout
arousing chills and so much more.
You light the chimenia, our lips unite
burning in the bottom of desire,
your touch intoxicates me.

The breath I feel
beneath the poncho liner
as we embrace the evening's ambiance,
your fingers like feathers on my skin.
The makeshift hammock that you strung
between two live oak trees
sways back and forth,
leaves fall as we succumb;
a gasp of breath in twilight's dawn
assures me that our love endures.

First Love

Jeff Newport

That Florida summer, the year
you moved in next door, we'd crawl

under the barbed wire fence
to meet each morning

in the hayfield,
prodded by some power

neither of us understood.
With clenched hands we'd

clumsily kiss, and in the faint
daylight return our

separate ways. Summer passed,
and now I can't even remember

your name.

The First Time

Victoria Slotto

The first time that I witnessed birth,
saw the crowning of the head,
that shock of thick black hair,
heard the melded cries of mother
and her son, the pain and ecstasy
in resounding dissonance,
the joy and fear and victory
of shattered boundaries—
that first time I beheld the
mystery of newborn life
I shuddered in the face of Awe.

The first time that I prayed in silence
without words or thoughts and stood
like Moses by the burning bush
that would not be destroyed and
offered (to the One who is and was
and will be) all that I have been and
am and shall become without limit
that first time I embraced
the mystery of divinity
I shuddered in the face of God.

The first time that I tasted love,
sought urgently to touch and hold,
looked into eyes that knew
my secret sacred spaces,
longed to please before receiving
pleasure, lost track of time, luxuriated
in the scent of passion,
that first time I received the mystery
of you, of all we could become,
I shuddered in the face of Bliss.

The first time I attended death
and held an old man's icy hand and
looked into his eyes that saw beyond
me, wiped a brow expressing
nuances of sorrow and of joy,
the scope of everything we can imagine,
that first time I received a dying breath
and closed those eyes
I shuddered in the face of the Unknown.

The last time that I said hello, goodbye
I shuddered in the face of Wonder.

wildfire—
ash on the wings
of a raven

Sandi Pray

whispering palms—
a heron's path
between stars

Sandi Pray

maple blossoms—
the scent of clouds
before the rain

Sandi Pray

Purls of Pearls

Laurie Kolp

I'm standing at the window looking out.
War and hate and death and fire and flood
are stitched into my mind, these words I sew
a clashing patchwork quilt with threads of blood.

But then I see a flash of red and blue,
birds sitting side by side beneath the seed
taking turns, respecting each winged space
as others peck at bark from Father Tree.

And all at once I'm filled with inner peace,
I know this moment here is everything.
No war nor hate nor death nor fire nor flood
can ruin purls of pearls sweet nature brings.

Word Wrapping

Susan Chast

You have a gift for unwrapping
not just the onion-like but too
the cocooned and folded in on

You are my idea un-wrapper,
not fooled by periods and dashes
nor led astray by ellipses, not trying

Open sesame and other magical
additions to the formula, just
sliding your being into openings

Words provide, accepting their
several ways into the house,
untie-ing welcomes at the doors

Cleansing Our Bibles

Charles David Miller

At the witching time I wake to find
what survived the day in fading dreams
that throw their shadows into distant light.

I eat nothing so that the pit in my stomach
can work its way into walk and talk
for my trip across the tight rope sky.

At the Jiffy Lube, a man with few teeth and a large smile
tells me he works 8 hours 7 days a week.
He's glad for Thanksgiving to come.

Once, at a laundromat, I accepted change from hands
with fingers cracked raw by chemicals.
He saw my horror and sighed.

If only I were stone I could endure not seeing.
If only I were a tree I'd know how to be.

The cold and bitter wind unweaves
a prayer's hem from my soul.
Let's write our own bibles,

revealing ourselves
to ourselves. We'll wash up clean
and remember to seek and erase the memory.

Doubt

Tiffany Coffman

When my God leaves me is when he comes in

Hot as a noonday demon

Perched atop a ventricle or two

Flooding the engine with blood and mud

Chirping squawking screeching

Digging them claws in

Checking the tension for weaknesses and barrier breaks

Cracks in the frame

Gunning it mother fucking loving it

Laughing at the tempered heat rising

Boiling over, out, in

Caustic gastric mother fucking fantastic

Chasing the shame of it all around the track

The bend, the break, the beast

Throat grabber

Voice nabber

Jibber jabber

Shh...

couleur des yeux: marron

Claudia Schoenfeld

you should never trust a scene
that seems all too tranquil, like
Paris between rain and sunshine,
& la Seine, winding lazily and shimmering
to the feet of well, a woman, (she looks
german or italian), and a lovely couple,
tourists probably— american,

i'm dressed in black,
drink café au lait in a place,
not far from Saint-Germain-des-Prés
marvel at stain glass windows
in a 12th century church with contacts
that i met some minutes back,
all peaceful, but

i'm on a mission, and late—

oh you should promenade
the streets of Paris, mingling with
Monet, Napoleon & Hemingway, inhale
l'esprit du capitale d'amour, bask
in her christmas lights— i run,
fall off the metro shaft,
M1 direction— di Ré Ction—??? mon dieu—
ahh— la défense— jump on the train,

only to wait hours on the messenger—
see, this is what it is about—

running, waiting, watching, listening,
soft clack clack of typing on the keyboard,
busy conversations on the phone in french,
i pick up bits and pieces, fill the blanks—
the printer slides state documents
across its glassy tongue—
a hoover hums, soft tic toc of the clock,

i catch the train to meet my colleague
on the exit of a windy station//just a minute
before midnite— hand him a brown envelope,

in a few hours he will board a flight—
"you'll be fine—", i kiss him three times on the cheeks
(that's what the french do) & report
"the only thing i shot was Notre Dame—"
(after admiring her for one short minute—)

she of course—
           was beautiful

the euclidean vector or my washing's sigh on sunday evenings

Claudia Schoenfeld

she sits bent over her exercise book,
vector analysis, on the table between dinner remnants
and a catalog, announcing spring,

& if i had a nougat colored blouse
with cappuccino dots, i'd put it on now,
in the meantime i dress black, (anyway, i'm useless
when it comes to shopping) &

my daughter nods "why would someone pay
300 euro for this bench? vintage. you could find one
in the bulk waste & just repaint" i clear away
the dishes, "so,

what exactly do you need the vector for?"
she shoots a pic of the solution, texts it to her friend,
shows me a video on YouTube to explain,

next to the table (way too close),
hangs today's washing, still
a little wet & crinkled on the rack, listening yawningly
to day's end whispers— with a deep sigh
shuts the eyes & freestyle (means:
no single peg), it dreams

    & dreams—

        & dreams—

           of spring

house on greenwood

Charles David Miller

A neighbor walks her spaniels at dawn
in the green park and orange light. A bullfrog
croaks alarm or desire near the pond where ducks glide.

On my walk to work, I pass a house
left empty by its black owners.
The overgrown lawn and old quarry stone steps
bid one long, lost welcome to friends.
They will not come again to drink beer,
grill brats, and sit in the shade of elms.
The for sale sign is a sign-post for lost worlds.

I've never set firmly my feet in this world,
or found the stillness of heart to plant
body and soul in earth. Like the lone firefly
announcing summer days ahead of its tribe,
I only brighten a night of loss.

Called to account,
perhaps bared teeth and claw
will slink from angled corners of my self,
those oblique shadows we cast unseen,
the blindness to what our acts produce,
the refusal to see who or what I was and became.

Blow the sparks
Easy stoke up the flames
Tame them with air

Blow the sparks

Mart Stel

Worcester Floods

Polly Robinson

You don't see them
But they are there.
Gulls: beaks gaping;
Cries raging; waiting for
Detritus from
The flood.

See the trees in deep water, stranded
They grow taller, stand staunch
Sentries of the flood.
Malvern Hills yawn,
They've seen it all
Before.

Low winter sun
Bejewels rising tides, a trance of
Wrinkles enhanced
On a cheekbone.
Laced branches reach for the roiling skies, advance,
Dip into the depths, drowning.

You don't see them
But they are there.
Gulls: beaks gaping;
Cries raging; waiting for
Detritus from
The flood.

Patty Melt

Mark Windham

She calls me "Honey" twice, "Sweetie" once —
the fat waitress with bad teeth, dirty nails,
sneezing while she refills peppershakers
while waiting for my order,
the Patty Melt.

Meat juices mingle with onions and cheese
stealing any crisp from the toast,
hash browns accomplish both crispy
and greasy.

Sunlight reflects a rainbow pattern in the
grease left on the plate.

The flies stay polite,
one scavenges the crumbs,
two scour the light fixture,
another patrols the thick air.

Unshaven, the old man at the counter
with me interjects himself into
the waitresses' conversation,
his hand trembles as he clings
to his coffee.

I pay my penance, accept a departing
affectionate honorific — "Honey" again —
return to the waiting day,
smells clinging
to my clothes like unwashed
sins to a soul.

is there a catch-line when it comes to saying thanks--?

Claudia Schoenfeld

train signals break night's eye,
hushed whistles, caught in thick high-voltage wires,
and—i—hang between them,
not like someone trapped though, or
kept prisoner, just moving a bit slower, pulling
softly from a place of warmth, light
glow of cheeks in certain pale-ness, swarms of
ions, pacing dark sky with a hand full of frail clouds aside— not
verified, or proven ground, just space to feel how
intimate you kiss within a room of healing,
nestled in calm pools of neon light,
"gotta go" i say, then hold your hand, for just another heartbeat

Distracted

Kevin Connelly

While attempting Poetry
at my desk one day,
fighting off the usual
bears, wolves
and other dangerous beasts
of the internet
between the Muse and Me;
from the teeth of Twitter,
a ferociously distracting
animal,
there leapt out
Billy Collins, Poet
talking of Poetry.
Losing myself
in his
captivating
flow of words
I ended
up Poetically satisfied,
but Poetically wishing
I had not been
ambushed
by dingoes of distraction
and had instead
written
a Poem.

ax battler

Saiqa Aftab

shadows slip into a time where you shut me out,
close me down,
devour our ours,
demolishing dreams around and about,
shout that you forget me,
eclipsing thoughts in tune,

refuting duty;
louder than saluting your beauty standing out in the crowd,
my intention was discretion at arms' length in truth not so easy,
chaos in a summer breeze edicts kissing me dizzy,
remembering a past tense not today love I'm busy,
i conclude: it was you,

shimmering in blue jewels making bonds breaking rules,
too much for me too less for you,
confused moves,
freezing moods,
distance is a curfew,
notes lost in transactions abused,

fall to my knees high on sugar syrup choking on rattled runes,
watching me squirm wishing you'd swoon,
underneath your skin,
sheltering within,
finding ways to be without you,
foolish whispers...

brush away the hair from my eyes,
you glint in my sunlight,
fingerprints on your smile,
your residue lets my mind stay a while
on a wish cast into a skimming wind,
inked out goodbyes written into gypsy sin,

king into oblivion in front of a million,
two divide by one remainder curses cast into mapped out domains,
my murmuring heart pollutes our imaginary conjectured pain,
cut veins / purple heart / bleeding sonata:

again.

Words Are Music

Rod E. Kok

Softly in the background
the music played.

Singers sang the words
that made the people
feel ... something.

Emotion brought on by
different voices,
the haunting tunes,
melody and harmony;
words that cut to the quick.

Chords were made alive
resonating through us all.

We didn't know that the notes
lived in us, through us.

Put your words to music
is what the writer wrote.

What notes need to be struck?
A dirge or a ditty,
how will it sound to those who hear?

What you say shows the bar
filled with halfs and wholes,
quarters and eighths.
Lines up, lines down,
it doesn't change the sound
of our words or the tune
that accompanies them.

Rest. Breathe. Sing.
Forte! Double forte!!

We long to be heard,
our passion is the sound
of our own voice.

Our love is tied
to what we speak.

Sing of love, of desire.
Sing with a smile.
Speak from the heart.

Write your song,
speak your heart.
Our words are music.

Snowfall

Mitisursus

There is something so forgiving about the snowfall,
laying over the Earth like a virgin-white wedding dress,
lovingly holding her in the embrace of a silence consummate
with the promise of renewal.

You go into the wilderness,
now all bedecked in uncrushable pearls
(each holding a little dust in its core)
and fluttering crystals formed as unchanging
expressions of the lovesong that conjures life,
lighter yet larger, harder and yet fluffier,
than the form that flows through life.
There is something so patient about the snow,
embracing her with whispered promises
certain as prayers in each of Heaven's frozen tears.

I know all the inexplicable losses in your memory:
Even in these formidably frozen hollows
of wilderness waiting through winter;
I see your hopes,
I feel the joyful dance with her,
as you swish her pristine wedding dress
that is adorned with all your light
that the crystals and pearls can reflect.

I feel the urgency of your love, a sunbeam
beating in your heart like a stag's hooves,
burning like the breath that condenses in the crisp air,
urgently longing for the sun to melt away these adornments,
giving safe passage to consummate renewal.

Have faith: Though all is changing,
Here, there is enough space of imperturbable quiet
to hear my infant whisper below hearing –
I am coming to be with you –
the snow whispers in the sound
of its twirling dance from the heavens
to swaddle all with silent promise.

Have no doubt
that Life will come again as it always has,
well prepared by pearls of promise
and crystalline songs that will become
the waters of spring.
The question is, will you dance again?

The snowfall gives you the silence
to make yourself free to be bound again –

in all the muddy muck of birth
when the winter wedding dress melts into her;
the snowfall gives pause
for the renewal of vows:
life will not be the same as before –
but all that you have lost will be contained within me, and all of your
        losses and she and you and I
will be whole again.

Creation's Flow

Delaina J. Miller

My eyes scan the face
pressed into the moon.
Death, ice cold and white
but only with the sun's touch.
Spheres float in gravity's pull
harnessed by invisible lines.
Parts of the whole, we are not cogs
but survivors by will.

The moon reminiscent of my dad's translucent skin,
pale as mortality sips the fire from his core.
Did he plant this creative flame? Did Mom?
Conception lit the wick, but the big bang
came from within.
This universe of words that flow
and tangle in my puppet strings
take the parts and create the whole.

opening the blinds
the eyes
of snowmen

Ben Moeller-Gaa

autumn wind
the neighbor's tree
becoming ours

Ben Moeller-Gaa

from the hammock
birds fade into crickets
crickets fade into stars

Ben Moeller-Gaa

Midnight

Ainsley Allmark

Midnight
A whispered prayer
Gossamer thoughts
Fragrant ideas born
Of things in shadowed memories

Shadowed memories of
Midnight
Ideas held suspended
In places
Where light seldom goes

Light plays
In fevered memories
Midnight
Times when old thoughts
Seldom play

Play the games
From when we were young
And dreamt that
Midnight
Was somewhere we could go

Somewhere in our thoughts
A secret place
We always held hands
And held the thoughts of
Midnight

Outcast|Alien|Refugee

Anthony Desmond

I wake up the moon
With shattering glass
Mirroring my mind state
Seven years bad luck
A devil child now a grown man
Whose untimely death
Will begin while
Burning in hell
That's the story of a human
Who came into this world
Just like everybody else
When the only piece of him
That was taken without permission
Was his foreskin
Now blood clots travel
To the heart of a monster
Metaphorically speaking
Like raising a stillborn child
To save on the funeral costs
Because that's what being
A decent american is all about

Passing off The Brain Dead As One of You

Anthony Desmond

The mockingbird that don't sing is you
The conformist is you
The loner with a bright future is you
The problem is you
The suicidal one who's all smiles is you
The life that flashed before
The pull of a trigger is you
The narcissist is you
The hero is you
The spineless snake is you
The advocate is you
The rebel is you

The process

The Missing

Joy Donnell

Weeks later
she would resign she'd lost her red silk thong forever.
While answering work emails, she imagined the airy crimson
victimized by crazy fates; [1] an unrealized bookmark
between pages
of Cancer
dusty
below an abandoned bed
[2] flapping along the flagpole of devout Communists
[3] deconstruction at the mouths of feral dogs, in an alley,
ruined;
but the montage gave way to a hope he still had it
its entirety enveloping his long fingers
and maybe while contemplating
its biography and the origin of the world
he closes his eyes
inhales.

A Quiet Drink With My Husband

Joy Donnell

– in his moonlit hands
a simple glass of bourbon
resembles the river Ganges
mythical and atoning;
within such mysticism,
I consider my own glass differently.
He watches me sip, warmly expand;
my side-eye makes us giggle.
Then,
the night is still again
so, we savor our gravity
just the moon
just our breaths
and breathless possibilities.

Birth

Robert Gerryts

How arrogant to think
the knitting stops
the day we leave the womb

A final loop
the knot is tied
a breath is drawn
a cry is cried
and everyone declares
the miracle is finished

But times will come
when souls are bruised
and ribs are cracked
when sorrow's mist surrounds
and grief knocks at the door

Through tears and pain and broken hearts
we will cry again

And...

...quietly you'll start to knit...
...calmly you will start to weave...
...slowly you will make us whole...

Because the miracle continues

flurries of willow fluff
seven ducklings scatter
among the reeds

Polona Oblak

becoming cold
a white butterfly drifts
into my dream

Polona Oblak

Poetry is my Herb

Christena Williams

Call it Kush
I smoke fifty bags in lines
Even hundred
Poetry is my herb
My vital remedy
Ignite
Burning
Smoke me up
And let the herb fumigate
And let its aroma fill the air
Poetry is my herb.

Why?

Shwetank Rana

I wonder why, O' deep blue sky,
your thoughts I cannot follow
How does it feel to be so high
yet never to cast a shadow

I wonder why, the sea is shy
to share its joys and sorrow
How can it be so sublime
and somewhere be so shallow

I wonder why, do people cry
Their hearts still seem so hollow
From endless tries, their eyes dried
to fool an innocent fellow

I wonder why, does time go by
never to bring tomorrow
Life is like a lucid lie
death may make us mellow.

sunrise trail—
whose song follows me
through the mist?

Sandi Pray

At War With Me

Dana Dampier

I have yet to breathe
Enough hours to rid
My mind of you

Acquiring enough minutes
To spend contemplating
Your soul

Defying every second
That your existence
Spills away

Fearing the day
You forever take leave
From my life

It's not possible for me to love you,
Yet I find myself trying

Photographing the Dead

Steve Shultz

Driving by the cemetery at night
just to know I'm alive.

Some say it's disrespectful to photograph the dead,
yet nobody's ever developed a soulless film roll.

Racking my brain about life's torture & rewards
— purgatory seems like such a nice idea.

Apps

Polly Robinson

Angry Birds ... AnGry birds
PiGs eat legs,
Birds protect eggs.
Pigs steal, man deals
Catapult bLow... stop,
STOP.

Twitter, twEEt, sharp # sweet,
ShaRp hashtag ...
Continuum,
Dominium,
Delirium, requiem,
Oblivion, weaRisome.

Cut the rOpe, amphibian,
Om Nom
SwiPes.
FeEd with candy,
Open mAw,
Je t'adore.

Over and Out

Steve Shultz

One toke
where is the line
toe it over and out
walking a tightrope out of sorts
free fall

Interconnect

ND Mitchell

Ice dystopia
Next in line for leaving home
Thawed heart if you speak.

Exhale winter through
Raindrop drumming on your mind
Carry on, dig deep.

One life left to leave
No one misses seeds you sow
Never for nothing.

Estimate your worth
Chasms cannot close themselves
Take your time my friend.

Quand Je Suis Avec Vous

ninotaziz

à la brune

la lune dans mes mains
mots d'amour tombe en silence
c'est ce que je ressens

quand je suis avec vous

nuit sera bientôt ici

***

questo è quello che sento quando sono con te

al crepuscolo
la luna nelle mie mani
parole d'amore

volano! Notte sarà presto qui...

***

senja kembali

purnama merindu
kata kata kekasih
membelai ku

tatkala bersama mu
malam berlabuh di tirai

***

at dusk

the moon in my palms
wings give flight to words of love
I sigh and tremble

when I am with you

Firegold

Jennifer Wagner

dusk
is a notion
of half-closed lids
in yellow flicks
of candlelight
against your bluegreen eyes
where
despite or because of
that lonely space between us
you pull me into
it
reaching for that tender
part you save for me
until i believe
i am the jewel
upon your hand
you always say i am
and melt like gold
in your palms

The Icarus Quandary

ninotaziz

Words – a trailblazer
Going out on a limb
Flying high

Lost, I fell
From paradise at the tip
Of a pen

Awaken!
the writer within
grasp your destiny

Understand
the turtle's song of regret
upon the waves

Tears like
pearls escaping from
a broken necklace

and dream
the dream of the pomegranate
a story within

each translucent seed of awareness.

for Nothing

Jane Davitt Hewey

I am waiting. Lowest bones settled on the chair's wooden edge.
Some call it meditation, but I know I'm waiting for absence
to replace these blue-laced waveforms and faceless angels.

Shoulders dropped in grave response, I soften the back of my neck.
Guardians, alchemists, Christ's Buddha caterwaul my pulse.
Inside and outside meet at right angles in my heart, sensations—
flame, hunger, even hope steps aside for this wait.

It is a selfish one; I've stood here stark naked, cells dividing
the penumbra between snow melt and mantle. Sat anxiously
kicking the dirt while the last leaves disintegrate. Everything
I've learned or loved was born of this stagnant, space-infused dearth.

not that I possess

Jane Davitt Hewey

my pulse awakened
to the awkward shadows huddling
under luxury's sufficient furnace.
I gave up trying to sleep

and watched streetlights
whisker through the blinds
onto your chin.

Thy Pulchritude

Shamsud Ahmed

Where do you want to go today?
Let me throw some sunlight on you;
Do you know the alleyways?
Let me guide you and hope the twilight stays.

You have come from a faraway land;
But I know that smell;
Even in the midst of storm and years – bygone,
I never lost you, though I was proved wrong.

Those crusaders are synchronizing their act.
And I might be their next prey;
I never longed for a life by this bay,
Dying for my love was always my way.

Let us count the minutes,
And break them into years;
Let me live thousands of decades with you,
Is it plausible? A few more days!

Shinwari

Susan Daniels

She squats, entombed already
inside that burka,
gray linen worn as the stones
and soil beneath her flat sandals

stares into the treeline, past it
her end playing out
away from that greenness
and silent, meeting it

but she is not stone
nor is he, not yet,
not completely,
because she flinches
and his hand shakes
as he aims and misses twice

her head up, not bowing
before four more shots
send this woman
who allegedly fell already
lower, the way flesh falls
when it no longer fights
inevitable things
like gravity.

Bare Bones Poem

Vivienne Blake

Dust dancing,
still, alone, silent,
glittering above,
reflecting below.
Choking in awe,
I hear music
as wind blows
the dust from my mood.

A Current Spare

S.E. Ingraham

String heart beats enough
Across the crack splitting
The chest; maybe temper
The racket thrumming there
Latch it closed against the draft—
It threatens to widen the chasm

Fingers numb-blue with trying
To hold sides together
Trace ragged edges sharp
Enough to draw blood's refrain
"Give it up, give it up"
Blend ignobly against a current
As spare as winter in Chernobyl

after putting the words down
they nudge each other
into place

Sondra J. Byrnes

menopause
where is
the pause button?

Sondra J. Byrnes

The Sounds of Time

Ainsley Allmark

Susurration
Sand between fingers
Sensuously
Slide

Slipping under feet
Sea kisses our toes
Sowing new memories

insanity

dani harris

insanity waits

at the dark edges of my soul

longing to embrace

Marigolds

Kathleen Gresham Everett

Marigolds always remind me of you,
I guess because you despised them so.
Were the flowers too ordinary or
their spicy fragrance offensive
to your superior senses?
Were their colors of yellow, orange, gold,
rust too garish for your discriminating taste?
Too bright, too gaudy, too common?
A lowly flower found in cheap seed packets
and blooming in less tasteful gardens,
their cheerful, happy countenance, a childish bouquet.

We were never the exquisite flower to place in your lapel,
marigolds and me.

Cotton Field

Kathleen Gresham Everett

I walk the gravel path
Along the field ready for harvest
The morning breeze
Catches the flags
In a steady percussion
I hear the pipes
As the tall black Percheron horse
Comes into view
Pulling its flag draped wagon.

I think of the old king
On his funeral bier
A country man, a veteran of foreign wars
Whose long reign
Kept the warring factions in an uneasy peace
Knowing that at his death
His kingdom would soon divide itself
Into civil and uncivil war.

I watch as the princes of your house
Bring you to your final resting place
And I know
That for the rest of my life
I will never see a field
In full and glorious cotton
And not think of you.

Finding Alone

Jane Davitt Hewey

Coupling with the gravity drawn by day,
my feet to sand on trail are winding low.
I hold one fear, too dear, in arm's length bay
that silent woods leak nothing left to know.

As fluttered wings may never want this pain—
wrought fully 'cross the sky with sea as mime,
can thrush to beech or stone to rock ledge gain
some handsome, burnished bush on twisted climb?

The view from here is better than I thought,
obstructed scheming plans are lynched and gone.
A nimble breeze holds freedom in a plot
for fantasies and fears to merge as one.

Height's barren, windswept landing sees me led
to peace in hand. My soul is deftly fed.

The Ocean

gennepher

She heard it in the echoes
of the rosary beads of memories,
be aware of words
beware of them.
Behind her eyelids she watched
illusion and reality,
the dance of life.
Paint peeling
the lighthouse sang an old song,
part of everything part of nothing,
unsettling the ocean.
A slender thing
what might have been,
hidden
for a lifetime.

Never Saw

Shamsud Ahmed

I have never been to the peaks,
I never saw the ocean,
Never been to the land where it resides.

The River – my companion,
Never saw the foundation,
I hope to see the end someday
Cause I plan to see the sea.

I never saw those eyes,
But I know the fear within;
Of loss and hardship,
When they sail on their warship.

I never knew that language,
But I can feel the odium;
I am the kill today,
Few more breadths, if escaped.

I will never see the snowflakes,
Nor the Ocean;
The River – Not my chum now;
In this tiny cell – my home now.

Waiting for my turn in isolation,
Darkness sometimes makes you look inside,
Sometimes makes you gather courage;
Courage to die, don't even know the time and age.

Lullaby of heartfelt longing

gennepher

On the golden stairs hands received
seagulls of space
flying between stars
wing-tip to wing-tip.
The past,
she held her secrets
letting them go one by one
into a garden of possibilities,
planted by you.
Snippets of memories
always hovering so near.
As the sun set,
the wind blew softly
whispering her real name,
and the lullaby began her search
on the blank white page of innocence.
Deep within,
the path wandered,
and the mouth asked a silent question.
No one answered,
so the wind blew gently
and carried the lullaby home.

The Choice

Kathleen Gresham Everett

Counting back to that first glance, seconds and minutes,
hours and years, the desire and candor of bodies,
when our days became charged with the pace of lives lived.
Years of longing renounce the yearning to another,
no longer young. The clamor of middle years
leaves satisfaction and knowledge in its place,
a quietness whose heft outweighs the struggles.
Wisdom is as wisdom does, patience is its own reward,
love never fails, never. And this is the choice,
made and kept, to choose you now and at each sunrise.
Until the day comes that my hand is not recognizable to you
And my laughter is silenced by your unknowing eyes.

No words for me

gennepher

I wonder
what time will bring
this spring day
catkins growing on the willow
love lonely so far away.
Today I stepped outside of me
cream silk rustling
as I dance
here on the island
just you and me.
From over the sea
mists roll in.

There are no words for me.

Song of Songs – There I Will Abide

Kathleen Gresham Everett

I

And there I will abide
Abide seems to be a word
filled with soft meaning
and deep intent
I will abide
Belong, rest, take comfort, dwell,
I will abide
Withstand, endure, await, sojourn
Accepting without hesitation
I will abide

II

My love is my abode
His limbs pillars of fragrant cedar
To shield me in my rest
His arms are oaks of sinew and might
Silver is on his head
Burnished and gleaming
Sapphire are his eyes
More beautiful than the morning sky
His heart is of precious stones
More valuable than the kings stores
He calls my name
And I am safe
My love is my love
And there I will abide

Reliquary

Kathleen Gresham Everett

As I sweep into my hand
from the table's edge,
the small sacrifices
you left for me,

I think about the saints
and their reliquaries.
Bits of bone
and parings,
faded cloth
and dusty splinters,
locked away in glass cases,
reflecting supplicants
kneeling in prayer.

Walking outside
under the dark heavens,
I release from my palm
the fragments of you
as the slender fingernail moon
rises brightly in the east

under evening's cloak
her sad song weeps
moonlight's child

gennepher

the colour of you
when I awaken
my dreams fading into night

gennepher

Hand in Hand

Ginny Brannan

Tenaciously, our hands embrace,
sweet nuance found in soft caress...
Emboldened, fingers intertwine—
with thumb on back of hand, you trace
against bare skin... feel a stir within...
in tethered warmth, I acquiesce.
Then quickened heart anticipates
through promises conveyed, unspoken;
and sharing secrets once repressed,
you whisper faintly in my ear
in language only love translates.
Our shadows dance along the wall
in a myriad of shifting shapes;
then palm-to-palm, your touch palpitates
to kindle fire, hand in hand.

Statued Statutes

Shane Stanisauskis

Freedom engulfs,

forests of fakery,
in flames of fury,
blame the jury.
Blatantly backward
but claiming surely
proclaiming the stance of master.
Faster, I race towards a pace of liberated factors
which propel me from slavery
into the hear, after.

Courts and societal stages
notoriety rages
upon the races of the young and aged.
Upon their faces,
emaciated traces
of abundance in hatred
and a lack of what's sacred.

While we waited,
they pushed their agenda,
the chances were slender
we'd ever remember.
Through indoctrination,
fake emancipation
illusions plaguing
the brains of a,
28 days later nation
intoxicated on,

viral asphyxiation,
A junkfood education.
The same level at graduation,
subjecting a generation
to excruciating payments.
I watch with a saint's patience
and ponder with galileo gazes,

With the rage of a billion men
On death row,
My breath slow,
Eyes bloodshot

with anger, towards said foe,
I watch, in amazement
as you
lose control,
as you lose control of me,
Internally combust at the thought of,

ME,
being free.
Your power gain,
was power loss,
at the cost of shots,
from my own pistol
firing,

blocked bullets in barrels,
blood upon apparel,
from erosive explosions,
eroding the fallacy,
fingertips slip
and tentacles drip
the hypnosis missed,
inside is the anarchy.
Inside is the animal,
The mammal I am.

Locked inside the clothes,
you impose upon man.
Locked inside the codes,
you impose upon man,
I oppose those frozen in courts upon man.
Legislative lies,
like licorice ties,

No more real than Lord of the Flies.
Pantomime time,
from nine until five.
Set stage up,
soldiers in line,
cogs grind,
but a lack of motion of those in mind
stand in line.
I decline the invite,
which entices consent of mine.

Caught in Your Deadlights

Ginny Brannan

How intricate those lies you spin—
well-shrouded in the perfect guise,
as subtly you hypnotize . . .

then soft, your touch against the skin
ever so light--until the bite
that paralyzes life within.

Your silken web now my demise,
entrapped within the lies you spin.

The Quarrel

Vivienne Blake

Pebbles crunched, whinged underfoot
as he prowled through achingly bright patches of light,
threaded by impatient wind and draggled clouds
darkening the sun.

Mewing, flapping gulls
streaked across the pewter sky above his head,
swooped on a deceptive piece of flotsam
then soared again, squawking their displeasure.

Desolation, blind to beauty;
no past, no future;
only the wretchedness of now.
His head-down plodding path continues.

A soprano trill
from along the shore
rouses him from misery.
She is there.

Totalitarianism

dom schwab

Having met them both before
and knowing how they were,
he had known (yes, he had)
how things would be if they would be,

and so he had crafted—had schemed—
a forward-looking plan
designed so he could move
undetected, safe from harm;

but, like a playwright's irony,
they uncovered unapparent inclinations—
positively base proclivities—the further
discovery of which would surely bring all to ruin,

and so he was checked, examined, checked again
until, at last (three years), he relented
and told them what they wanted:
"I don't think like that anymore."

The stroke grew
Through his limbs
In blackened death

Frank Watson

Subway to the Center of the Earth

Frank Watson

Groaning men
and tracks

of women who know
the carnal gaze

of tattooed jazz
in deep bass

as we're heading down
a heated core

the violent shore
of tribal pound

a prophet's sound
that says...
              we're
                  m
                e
               l
                t
                 i n g

down a hole
of earthly flesh

with three stops left

Notes for a Book of the Dead

Charles David Miller

1

I heard the dead whine like a bobcat in the pasture field.
Like a baby crouching in the grass near the springhouse
when the harvest weighs heavy on the stalk
and dew soaks your shoes.

Grandfather strode like an initiate of an earth goddess
down the country road with a wet-born calf in his arms.
Grandmother cut dawn's darkness with her flashlight
The air charged with magic and primordial calm.
The valley alive with mystery time alone can breed.
Binding together wheat stalk and hay bale
and mocking the hours like a catbird on the limb.

The dead disappear and are seen no more.
Their work rusts in the yard and their gardens decay.
Their eyes do not pierce the neon lights from the other side.
Their statues sweat no blood.
What they said is lost (no less what it meant).
A black car drove up and took them off.
They walked the trail of tears and bore the pain.
They died without name and address.
Some loved. Others hated and despised.
(Better dead and not remembered again)
No one to find them in their city lost to time.

The unspeakable crimes unsaid and unavenged.
There are no sacred words to open death's doors.
The dead seek rest and remembrance
on the tongues and in the souls
of the sick and diseased and hound their dreams.

2

Along the fragile mud banks
wailing boy and pouting girl
follow bloody spoor and echoing, hungry cry
from sheepfold to grave,
where the young god lies entombed.
Rice bowls are empty in temple gardens
as the vulture soars in ritual helix down the sky.
In drought time at the festival of light,
king and bride join in sanctuary bed.

The people huddle at the dry river banks
and pray for flood tide, life-quest and rebirth.
In the land between two rivers,
death gives birth to wisdom.
The dead embark from valley steps
to the land of the sun,
and the true measure of life
is not how many men you killed or slaves
serve you in the next world
but whether you hurt anyone or not.

The stations of the modern underworld bear sounds
like Treblinka, Auschwitz, Dachau, Bergen-Belsen.
The hieroglyphics of the book of our dead,
starkly naked, brutal depicting our nothingness.
The animal unveiled beneath pince-nez.
The angel slashed, burned, gouged, gassed, and shot.
A thin hand raises a cigarette to parched lips.
Toothless mouths gum green bread from the pit pigs swill in.
Lurid pictures obscene in their cruelty,
no mystery. The human husk ripped open without shame.
Spread-eagled legs bent back. Throat crushed.
The raped soul shot nude for postcards
the possessed will buy.

3

In my prayer to compassion's God,
to what high place should I climb
for those who died forgotten by us?
The past just a trick of words and memory.
Cut wounds deep in flesh.
Bury the tokens under moss and roots,
and ask forgiveness for not being there
in the terror that should be shared.

Where the walls are scrubbed clean
and bone shoveled into the common urn,
light a candle for the dead
where they watch from crumbling photographs.
And do not forget the winter night
that splintered like crystal on the streets
when the radio called them into the open maw
of factory gate and shower and bitter flame.

Time cannot fill the vacuum they left.
The dead need remembrance in rites
that strip bare the soul and throw it
to the ground in tongues they speak to us.
A language that solves all riddles and crimes.
That unmasks the sham and lie of the daily routine,
and leads truth seekers to open the graves
that schoolbooks do not write about.
For those who drank at the pit's lip
and sank into mass graves,
whose naked bodies the pictures show,
flesh melting into flesh in a dirt hole.

I ask to be like those who came out of it
and see now beyond death's frontiers.
Who saw new life root in ruins.
Whose breath once choked on hope.
Who put a knife to the camp guard's throat
but let him go when wrath
and suffering became a vision of dignity
uninvoked by gore on human hands.

And who, when ecstatic cry fills the room,
open the door at night to the tomb
and bring bright linen shrouds
to those who died cold, unclothed, and unjustly.

A Bed of Dollar Bills

Anthony Desmond

Death wears a crown
Set with a golden dove
Surrounded by gems in
Blackened blood burgundy
Such headgear holds the image
Of a halo and the weight
Of a lifeless vessel
Like guilt upon the shoulders
Like the ruby eyes of a bird

Tuaim Inbhir

Anonymous, translated from Celtic by Mario Brian O'Clery

No faux-Tudor blight might outdo
My Ivied Tuaim Inbhir bedsit,
Luminous stars lining
Its sun and its moon.

Gobbán Construction turned the sod
But you know how that went
And someone's God
Thatched it in the boom.

Bullets cannot touch me there,
Rain falls past
My bright orchard
Where no fences loom.

From the ninth-century monastic verse "Suibhne Geilt"

July '73

Mario Brian O'Clery

Coveting claw hammers on a warm garage Saturday,
Bending ovals in the rock sweet iroko
Below bursting dust tadpoles
While Daddy slurped his tea next door.

Then nail to nail broken
As the dull shudder trundled
Over corrugated waves,
History falling on the bitumen above

I dropped the hammer, running guilty
Through the lines of webbed ammunition cases
Drilled in uniform beneath the lathe,
Turning in the splintering wake

'That's a bomb' Tom called 'Get in'
Some giant shard of Wolseley axle skirting,
Scratching, piercing towards the bridge.
Stomach light in the storm's dead core.

I could hear the bees again, warbling.
Harmonised by armoured jeeps, converging.
'I hope nobody's hurt' said Willie Fox, emerging
But he knew, we all were.

Black Africa

Wale Owoade

I stood at the window
Of your dreams,
Overseeing your future
From your docile past.

Black Africa!
You have left
The truth at back
When rushing to buy
A bowl of lie.

Today......

Your world is black;
Black dreams, black light
Black luck, black truth.

Tears and cries;
Cries and tears—
All bound in unison
To run your smile away.

Isn't today the changing of time,
When fishes will know
The bait-worm on the hook?

Then........
Why beat the drum
To the master's humming sound
When you can dance your feet
To the drum beat of your old man?

Change

Wale Owoade

When my Africa dance,
She dances the dance
Of the warriors who builds
My home with their
Blood on my naked soil.

When my Africa dance,
She dances the dance
Of the wars who free
My home with their
Scars on my naked soil.

When my Africa dance,
She dances the dance
Of the gods who guide
My home with spirits
On my naked soil.

But today,
When my Africa dance
In the front of those
Modern city lights,
You shove your head out;
Out of your motoka,
Gnash your teeth
At the jejune sight
Beholding your civilized eyes.

Your Priest shakes his head,
Sorry for the unholy stranger
In front of his sacred realm
And prays: 'Dear Lord
                To this mad woman
                Please grant a relief!'

Happy 48th Independence Day, Gambia!

Sheikh Ahmed Tijan Bah

On this day, past forty-eight years,
Our leaders carried the country's fears;
The people took the Motherland on their shoulders,
And marched, to the sky, as soldiers.

Forty-eight years now going,
Still strong, still growing—
The flag is flying high
And yet to reach the sky.

So much has gone astray,
But the Motherland will stay—
And many have gone,
But still more are born.

Life continues,
The young reissue—
But as the Motherland grows older,
Will the young take her on their shoulders?

raven shadows—
the mountain inclines
towards dusk

Sandi Pray

starry night—
the ebony of her eyes
and the moon

Sandi Pray

Quilt

Rosemary Nissen-Wade

I made it when my kids were small.
It lay on our queen-size bed
all the further years of that long marriage.

Not your neat, traditional crochet squares
but larger, lacier, the pattern
more complex. I was proud

of this persevering work of my hands:
a fine thing, a whole year to make.
I loved its rich, strong colours.

It was variegated green, emerald to sage.
It was two tones of red, intense
and understated. And the wide borders

were black. I thought they gleamed
with power and love. The top, defined
by wider black, turned back over the pillow.

After the marriage ended in tears,
I folded the quilt away in a cupboard ...
bundled it off at last to the charity shop.

What comfort could it be to my old age?
Rage had turned it ugly in my sight.
Grief had made it lie too heavy on me.

Now I live in a warm climate. I like
the Indian cotton throw I bought:
lighter, freer, matching my present love.

Taking the Obs

Rosemary Nissen-Wade

Around his neck, under his pyjama top,
a white plastic rectangle hangs from tapes.
It has a dial with lights and symbols
which the nurses can decode. 'We think
it might be your ticker causing the falls.'

They take his blood sugar, more often
I suspect, than the twice a day
I've been doing at home. And they take
blood pressure, temperature, pulse, all that.
They check his water, intake and output,
and whether his bowels have opened today.

I am a visitor now. I must relinquish him
into other care than mine. I am training myself
not to ask what his blood sugar is this time,
nor at what hour they gave his insulin dose.
'He's in good hands,' the nurses reassure.
'You've done a wonderful job,' says the doctor.
'It's enough! Time to let us look after him now.'

Only last week, when I started a cold,
he was the one looking after me,
wrapping his warm arms around me,
stroking my hair, soothing me off to sleep.
I examine, now, as he lies in his hospital bed,
the smile in his eyes as we share a joke,
the interest in his voice as he asks the nurses,
'Where did you grow up? Where did you train?'

I observe the way his hair curls over his ear.
I watch his hand take hold of mine. I perceive
the gentleness of his touch, the warmth
of his loving clasp. I monitor not the beat
but the inclination of his heart, its directions;
I try to gauge his happiness levels, his peace.
This has been my chief occupation for years.
I can't stop noticing and caring, just because
he's now in a hospital, being clinically observed.

The Goodbye Ritual

Rosemary Nissen-Wade

On the night of the full moon last
I did the ritual —
I called the Powers to witness
my long-delayed, formal goodbye
to the dear man who has gone into my past.

Not that I could see the full moon.
It was utterly black, that sky —
not even pin-prick stars.
Heavy, relentless, the rain fell and fell.
Light would not pierce that veil, not soon.

So I came indoors,
and from far and high
I called them all —
the elements, the God, the Goddess —
into my bedroom, which used to be ours.

And there I said goodbye to my beloved;
a final, deliberate farewell
within a circle of sacred space,
watched by the moon's invisible eye ...
admitting at last that he is dead.

Goodbye to my Grandfathers

Tom Swanston

Mollycoddle – that's a word my grandfather taught me,
Or, at least, he would have done had I known him.

They say that you can't miss something
That you've never known,
But I miss my grandfathers.
I miss their big, wrinkly hands
Picking me up out of the sea as the waves
Crush the sandcastle that we have spent hours
Building together.

I want to so say farewell to my grandpa,
And adieu to my grandfather,
But I'm not sure you can say 'goodbye' to someone
To whom you have never said 'hello'.

Shakti

Patricia Costanzo

my thoughts have left this room
darted deep into a land
where play is an everyday occurrence

her body lies limp and youthful
gauze gown spread across
the daisy buttoned grass

once lifeless with inattention
her lips now curl sweet
black lashes slowly unfurl

the famished goddess wakes
dines on fairy tales
and from lilies drinks deep

roused by the scent of one worthy
unrestrained she stirs
choose now or leave her lie

for her powers grow quickly
if left to lust upon – your
mind's eye

Sometimes (Unsweetened)

Karin Gustafson

I sometimes understand that we'll all die,
without last try-again.
No refill of siphoned sand,
do-over (do what we can).

And that I too, and all I love, will die.
And my cry does not call
like the mourning dove, a fall/
rise, but has no interval.

Departure

Kelvin S.M.

when i hear
        rainfall

i think
        i already know

why the crickets
        do not sing.

a snowflake falls --
the morning blooms
like white poinsettias

Mary Grace Guevara

(Excerpt from Guevara's "Peace Haiku")

Z–A: Rebel Teacher Manifesto

ND Mitchell

zone in the zealless
year on year
(e)xcavate the x-factor and
walk with the weak.

voice the voiceless
understand the uninitiated and
try to teach tolerance.

share sunshine as you shoot down the shameless,
receive the reckless,
quieten the quarreler.

practise peace:
offer openness
nurture the needy (as you)
motivate the mocker (and)
learn to live with losing.

keep calm.

jettison the juvenile,
invite the ill-at-ease inside to invert the introvert.

hand out hope as homework. heal hatred.

guard the grateful
forgive the foolhardy
enliven the effortless; educate the eager.

deactivate the defeatist; defuse the derogatory; disarm the destructive;
drive their dreams.

choose to challenge the challenging and
battle to break down bitterness.
alleviate anger: absolve the abuser; advocate for the abused.
(and after all this: be the architect of their ambitions, the artist of their
aspirations...)

You know the toilet paper is cheap when you get paper cuts

Brian Miller

Will Robinson! Will Robinson!
it's time again,
DANGER! DANGER!

& truth be told you can find it anywhere,
even going to the bathroom

        (if you know what you are
                    doing.)

his sister sits in a padded chair,
among the mothers waiting to pluck
children from the bowels of classrooms
when the bell rings (when the bell rings!)

it's been a year since they fired me,
(you can't counsel when the client is unwilling
or the guardian no longer wants accountability)

'how's your brother doing?'

'oh hi, he's great. at home with mom, home
schooling now, still out in the woods
every chance he gets.'

'that's great to hear.'

'yeah your time with him did wonders.'

'i appreciate that. they still down
in Alta Vista?'

'yeah.'

i let her go, her stepson running
the shiny tiles---glad there is still space between us,
the last thing we did before was report her brother
to the authorities. on the way to the store,
he casually looked at me, deadpanning

'wouldn't it be fun to have a sniper rifle
on top of the Walmart.'

yes,
 yes,
    YES, Will Robinson, it's time to run,
DANGER, DANGER, DANGER
walks among
us, unchecked---& they fired me
for telling someone.

midnight train—
a whistle the length of
late night blues

Sandi Pray

turquoise water . .
a web of sunlight
behind my eyes

Sandi Pray

december's girl

Kelly Letky

I am the wraith of winter
I spin loose tales of death and direction
decorate with grey and hollowed out stones

I light the night with moondust and parody
weave rough wool from forest and folly
paint the sun into places you've never imagined

I can warm your toes and chill your heart
breathe life into howls that could tear you apart
sit silent when you beg for a song

I wear a belt of keys but never open a door
rattle chains that were forged from lost days
hope is the ring I wear on my finger

I am always gone and never away
neither friend nor foe in your subliminal story
I am the wraith of winter

mountain snow—
only the red sound
of a hawk

Sandi Pray

winter grasses—
the space between
your footprints

Sandi Pray

Nigori

Steve Shultz

Entire bottle
of sake gone;
  mind still cloudy

Rain

R.H. Mustard

The rain
has stopped,
gone somewhere
a long way off.
The world's asleep,
darkness filling
every corner.
In the stillness,
I listen for a reason
why we are here,
lying awake
each night
in the quiet, hearing
rain, far off thunder,
knowing we cannot
see beyond tomorrow,
never forgetting
the sound and the fury,
its approach forever
meant to warn us,
coming through
so loud, so clear.

When it was raining while the sun shined...

Sreeja Harikrishnan

Rising up high, birds spread their wings,
soft sunny rays, and a light drizzle on the sprigs,
this morning is beautiful, more than the rest.
Like tears and smiles, adorning a child's face,
when he gets back the marbles that he lost.

Nimi is happy watching all those leaves washed with rain, those drops dripping with a golden shine. When she saw her Mamma coming, she embraced and kissed her Mamma's cold cheek. "Mamma, you always sweat, and your cheeks are cold. You are always busy; when do you get time to enjoy, like I am doing now--- see the beauty outside." Mamma, pulling her child closer, said that she sees all the beauty in her little girl's eyes. Nimi smiled and said, "Mamma, you are like this morning, warm and showering." Mamma said to her little girl that she will tell a story on why there is sunshine on some days when it is still raining.

There was a simple man with a humble life,
he loved the girl next door, as he would love life.
He loved every pebble and cloud and everything
that he believed god has made, from his own blood.

"Did she love him, Mamma?" Nimi asked with wide eyes. Mamma said that the girl was silent, for she was the daughter of a rich man and never believed that they would ever unite. Nimi's face saddened, and she looked on to her mother's face, which was like god's message to her, where she searched for every answer she wanted. Mamma continued with her story.

He saw himself in her slightly moist eyes,
and when she passed by, he knew the fragrance
that took him to the deepest corner of his heart;
Where he felt the entire ocean and the mountains,
                            on earth.

Their love grew like the silence before a storm,
And like the fall before the rise of ocean waves,
And like the gloominess before the first rush of rain,
And spread like an unheard melody that was silent!

"Mamma, are you going to make me sad?" Mamma said that she wouldn't make her sad, but ardent like the wind and moist like nature on a rainy day like this. She would like her girl to be sensible and alive to every moment, so that she sees the persistence of the ants when they raid her kitchen, and feels the ache of a hungry beggar who comes to her, and sees the woman in her maid – that she will always keep her feelings as honest as her mamma's love. Mamma continued her story.

He never cried but smiled simply,
his smiles flew like birds, up, up and up.
But they rained heavily,
    nourishing every grass;
as they were so full with love
    and couldn't just be vapor.

Nimi gazed into her mamma's eyes and saw everything through her words. It was now raining heavily outside. The sunshine slowly drifted to its secret resting place. Water pooled on the ground, and rain drops fell on them, splashing all over.

The village was the land of farmers;
floods were their biggest rivals.
One day it was raining heavily;
another flood was impending.
The young man on his way saw the gap;
a gap, in the barrier that saved the farm,
he was the first to see, so he was destined
to fill the gap, and he jumped into the gap
 and filled the gap, with himself; so he blocked
the flood from rushing into the farm.
He filled the rest of the space with mud;
every other person who came afterwards
filled the gap by putting more mud,
as was the law,
and when the farmland was saved,
the young man was immortalized.

"Mamma, all his love lost?! This is so sad, what happened to the lady? Oh I can't take this, Mamma; they hadn't even shared a word with each other... total failure, nothing gained." Mamma continued her story.

No, my child, a whole village was saved
The farmland was saved, the livelihood
of many, and who said his love was lost?

The lady heard it, and she rushed like another flood
to where her heart was buried, deep under the mud.
The whole village witnessed how she hugged the mud,

how she cried, that even the rain stopped and watched
in awe.
Her love shone like ember on her face.
And her heart spilled like rain to the mud,
where her beloved was buried, deep under the mud.
All that was saved in silence was pouring out;
her grief was so unbearable that the sky fetched her up,
to the divine bosom, from where she looks down
with glowing love and raining grief.
Whenever hearts grieve over untold love, down here,
she showers her golden rays and soft drizzle,
Just to make those hearts ardent.

*"Mamma, this is touching, but what is it worth when there is no gain?
Yes, of course the young man is brave and saved the village, but the
poor girl has lost her love, and this rain shows her unfulfilled dreams."
Mamma smiled and stroked her girl's soft curls that adorned her
forehead. She looked out, and now there was sunshine again.*

Nothing, my child, in the whole world
is worth attaining! The moment you
feel your heart beating, and know the love
that is flowing, all around – that is worth eternity.
This is the moment, for which he sends us down
to bring him back the pearls of love, moist,
that he scattered throughout the universe, in his euphoria.

*Nimi gazed on her mamma with great love and embraced her. "And
when will all the pearls be collected, Mamma?"*

As many drops as there are in an ocean;
as many stars as there are in the sky,
so many are the pearls of his love.
And not many return with those pearls
                              to his abode.

*Nimi's eyes shined in the sunlight that spread to their room, through the
open window.*

Poet Biographies

ADDIE PETER ABBOT. An aspiring poet from the Caribbean island of St. Lucia, Abbot moved to Sheffield in England to study aerospace engineering. He loves poetry and has always loved writing. He wants to share his story with whoever wants to listen/read and tries his best to bring something new to the table with everything he writes, encouraging people to look outside the box. Currently he is an undergraduate student, and his favorite poet is Rudy Francisco. His poems are his Life, and he welcomes readers into it.

SAIQA AFTAB. A British-born Muslim, Aftab grew up with English novels and tales of Arabic myths, escaping the humdrum of the West Midlands. With a strict upbringing, secretly writing poetry allowed a balanced sanity in a sheltered world. Saiqa Aftab completed a B.A. in English Literature with honors, avoiding all the poetry modules to major in critical theory and aesthetics.

SHAMSUD AHMED. An accomplished poet, Ahmed has authored many books, including *I Am Dirty; I Need Washing*, which has been critically acclaimed and has received an overwhelming response from readers. He has been writing poems and short stories for local journals and newspapers for a long time. His recently published book, Rousing Cadence, is a collaboration with various poets across the world. These days he is busy scripting for a primetime TV show Jindagi.Com, which is on air via Rang TV. You can see more of his work at his website (shamsud-ahmed.com).

AINSLEY ALLMARK. Allmark lives in the beautiful west of Cornwall, UK, and has been writing poetry for very many years. He has been inspired by many things, including but not limited to location, people, and the workings of his mind. More poems can be seen at his main blog (dolphin-muse.blogspot.co.uk).

JOHN ANSTIE. Educated as a scientist, Anstie worked in engineering and commercial roles for the special steels and IT industries, including owning his own business. His muse landed in 2009 after forty-two years in a creative desert, pursuing a career and raising a family, which informed his writing. Among the poets who inspire him most are Shakespeare, for his use of the English language; John Clare, for his brilliance in spite of a lowly education; W B Yeats, for his romantic lyricism; Simon Armitage, for his undeniable, down to earth appeal; and John Updike, for his lyrical but rooted storytelling. Anstie lives in Sheffield, England, and maintains two blogs, writing rants and pants on Forty Two, his prose blog (poetjanstie.blogspot.co.uk), and poetry at My Poetry Library (poetjanstie.wordpress.com).

RICHARD ARCHER. For many years Archer has tried to make sense of a lot of things he sees everyday by making them into poems.

SHEIKH AHMED TIJAN BAH. Bah hails from the city of Banjul in the West African state of Gambia. He is currently pursuing a Bachelor's of Technology in Mechanical Engineering (B. Tech ME) in Sharda University, Greater Noida, India.

MARGARET BEDNAR. A wife and a mother of six children, three dogs, two cats, and one horse, Bednar currently lives in North Carolina, USA.

KATHERINE BISCHOPING. A sociology professor at York University and a playwright whose works have been performed in Toronto's Scotiabank Nuit Blanche and in the Humber River Shakespeare Company's Sonnet Show, Bischoping is partial to the voices of Matthew Arnold, Stevie Smith, and Virginia Woolf.

VIVIENNE BLAKE. Blake is a 74-year-old grandmother living in rural Normandy in France with her retired dentist husband. In precarious health, she writes as much as she can to cram in as much as possible in the time available (vivinfrance.wordpress.com). Her time is divided between family and friends, writing and quilting. Apart from two years living and working in Seychelles immediately prior to retirement, she hasn't done anything out of the ordinary. She started writing poetry 5 years ago with the first of four wonderful Open University creative writing courses. Having left school at 16, she is immensely proud of the fact she made it onto the stage in 2010 to receive her B.A.

GINNY BRANNAN. Brannan resides in Ludlow, Massachusetts, with her husband, son, and two cats. Inspired and encouraged by her best friend, she started writing poetry in 2009. She writes both formatted poetry and free verse and maintains a blog (insideoutpoetry.blogspot.com), and she enjoys reading Longfellow, Poe, Dickinson, Plath, and especially Robert Frost, all of whom are connected to her native New England.

RHONDA L. BROCKMEYER. A Canadian poet and artist currently residing under the Northern Lights in Edmonton, Alberta, Brockmeyer grew up in the wilds of farm country Ontario, near Owen Sound. She writes poetry and short stories. You can find her writing on her site (rhondalbrockmeyer.wordpress.com) and follow her Twitter alter ego @VespersAria.

ALI BROWN. From Newcastle upon Tyne, UK, Brown has always been drawn to writing and poetry, but started writing on a daily basis after the death of her mum in 2005. It was almost like a form of therapy in helping her to work through the grief. Brown draws inspiration from what she observes in every moment. As well as a writer, she is a counsellor, meditation teacher, and Reiki healer. She lives with her daughter and their cat, Tabitha.

GLENN A. BUTTKUS. Managing several vocations in his life, from professional actor to special education teacher, the only through-line for Buttkus throughout those turbulent decades has been writing. Two unpublished novels gather dust on dark basement shelves. The stanchion of his creativity has always been poetry, scribbling at it for fifty years. Having overcome luddite status a few years ago, his writing has blossomed into an outpouring of mind magma, and the loquacious networking of world class poets one finds daily at dVerse Poets has energized and challenged him delightfully.

SONDRA J. BYRNES. Byrnes is relatively new to writing poetry. It started two years ago when she realized that Twitter was a good forum for short-form poetry. She writes haiku, senryu, tanka, and other micropoetic forms. Her poetry has been published in *Tuck Magazine*, *Prune Juice*, and *Multiverses*; it is also included in *Fragments* by Blue Flute. Byrnes is also interested in ikebana, chanoyu, and sumi-e painting. She is a retired law and business professor from the University of Notre Dame and lives in South Bend, Indiana.

BRIAN CARLIN. Carlin is 54, from Glasgow, Scotland. He has worked as a psychiatric nurse for the past 25 years and has been writing for the past 10 years or so. From early doodlings to the present, Carlin's concerns have been how to reconcile words with the actual nature of things, and the mystical nature of that relationship. He also struggles to find a language which relates personally to his childhood but can be communicated with the outside world. Poets cherished are william carlos williams, early Pound, and Larkin for their clarity, and of late, the great Francis Ponge and some of the latter-day French poets who seem to share his sensibility.

SUSAN CHAST. Retired from a teaching ministry in 2012, only to fall smack dab in love with writing, Susan Chast has two blogs about poetry (susanspoetry.blogspot.com; susan60.blogspot.com). She lives in Philadelphia, Pennsylvania.

TIFFANY COFFMAN. Coffman lives in Arizona and began writing poetry at the age of 10. It was not reading that got her into poetry but rather a love of music. As a teenager, she was heavily influenced by Kate Bush's work as her poetry showed her what was possible. She has since taken her love for music and blended that notion of imagery, rhythm, and flow into her own writing. To Tiffany, poetry is music and should sing in your heart upon every read.

KEVIN CONNELLY. A native of Kilkenny City, Ireland, currently living in Duncannon, Co. Wexford, Connelly is an award winner in The Black Diamond Poetry Competition. He has had both poetry and flash fiction published as part of the Writers on Board Scheme of the Carnegie Library in Kilkenny. He has read poetry in the Wexford Arts Centre as part of the Cáca Milis Cabaret and on "Imeall," the Arts programme on TG4. Kevin regularly reads his work at Harry's Bar, Langtons Hotel (Kilkenny), and in The Fusion Cafe (Wexford). He publishes a literary blog (connellykevin.wordpress.com). A love of words brought him to poetry; Garcia Lorca, Elizabeth Bishop, Patrick Kavanagh, Roger McGough, Seamus Heaney, Robert Frost, and numerous others kept him there.

DANA DAMPIER. A mom to three boys by day and a poet by night, Dampier also writes a little flash fiction. She began writing poetry in the 3rd grade and immediately fell in love with words. She resides in Central Louisiana with her family. You can read more of her poetry on her blog (crazypoeticlife.com).

SUSAN DANIELS. A poet, parent, and gardener, Ms. Daniels lives in Western New York.

ANTHONY DESMOND. A twenty-one-year-old Detroit-born published poet/writer now residing in Center Line, Michigan, Desmond is intrigued by affliction & sadness and explores these emotions across a wide array of subject areas: politics, death, the hypocrisy of religion & the struggles of everyday life. Anthony believes in testing the limits of the permissible; his poetry is honest, unadulterated & breaches the norms of the expected. Desmond's poetry (sometimes credited as Anthony Scott) can be found in many magazines and books, including *What is Inspiration: Thoughts on Life Series Vol. 1*, *Railroad Poetry*, *The Rusty Nail*, *Tuck Magazine*, and *Signal from Static*, the epic collection of modern poetry from Chromatopias, LLC. He also shares work on his blog (glassstaircase.blogspot.com).

PRIYANKA DEY. Pursuing her Master's in History from Delhi University, Dey is a prolific poet. Her poetry is mostly available through online forums, and her blog (priyankazneverland.blogspot.in) is a virtual stream of poems. Though her artistic soul embraces other art forms, words have always been her first love. The language she uses is that which relates to the layman, but which is nurtured by the ethos of the Indian as well as global culture. Presently, she is also working on her first full-length novel. Her works have been featured in more than twenty anthologies, and she is the managing editor of a literary magazine in India. She is a die-hard optimist and a hopeless romantic. Her favorite poets are Sylvia Plath and Rumi.

JOY DONNELL. A writer, producer, and former publicist living in Los Angeles, Donnell has been anthologized in works published by Beacon Press, Random House, and Alyson Books. Her collection, *Angry Naked Mysterious*, will be released in Autumn 2013; check her website (doitinpublic.com) for more information.

FRANCES DONOVAN. Donovan's work has appeared in *PIF Magazine*, *The Writer*, and *Perimeter*. She curated the Poetry@Prose reading series from 2009–2010 and joined the Workshop for Publishing Poets in 2012. She lives in Boston, Massachusetts, with one human and two cats. You can find her online at www.gardenofwords.com.

KATHLEEN GRESHAM EVERETT. A writer and poet living in the Missouri Ozarks, Gresham Everett has self-published one volume of poetry, *The Course of Our Seasons*, and is currently working on her second. She writes on her blog of the same name (thecourseofourseasons.com).

gennepher. Travel is important, not the journey's end. Mostly gennepher writes haiku and gogyohka. However, she writes longer poems as well.

ROBERT J. GERRYTS. Husband, father, teacher, farmer, and writer by day – and completely exhausted by night – Robert Gerryts began writing in his early twenties and cellared most of his work for 20 years to let it age. He has only recently begun to release it to the wild, with more of his work found on his writing blog (everyonelisten.com).

MARY GRACE GUEVARA. "Writing is my creative corner, an outlet outside of work and real life challenges." A late bloomer in writing and blogging (since winter 2010), Guevara is self-taught in writing poetry and prose, relying on poetry communities like dVerse to sharpen and enhance her craft and appreciation for words. When she is not writing, she is Mom to 4 children (including the devoted hubby) and currently works as a financial analyst for an insurance company in Toronto, Canada. Guevara runs two blogs: as Grace in Everyday Amazing (everydayamazin.blogspot.ca) and as Heaven in Sweet Lust (a-sweetlust.blogspot.ca)

KARIN GUSTAFSON. Blogging as Manicddaily (manicddaily.wordpress.com), Gustafson focuses (sometimes) on the interface between creativity and stress. She is a writer and illustrator, having published a collection of poetry, *Going on Somewhere*; a children's counting book, *1 Mississippi*; and most recently *Nose Dive*, a light-hearted mystery novel about teenagers, Broadway musicals, love, noses, New York. (More information about the books may be found at BackStrokeBooks.com and Amazon). She is very thankful to the dVerse Poetry Pub for inspiring a lot of new poetry of her own and also for introducing her to a group of wonderful online poets. Follow Gustafson on Twitter @ManicDDaily.

SREEJA HARIKRISHNAN. From Kerala, India, Sreeja blogs regularly (writingonjusttowrite.blogspot.com). She loves painting and reading, which led to her love of poetry. It is tough to make the choice about a favorite poet; everyone is amazing. Maya Angelou's words are so inspiring.

dani harris. You can find more of Harris' poetry at her blog (myheartslovesongs.com).

JANE DAVITT HEWEY. Hewey (janehewey.net) lives in Seattle, Washington, and wakes up to beauty several times a day.

vb holmes. Editor, writer, and researcher, holmes is now also the author of an early nineteenth-century tale: *Reverberation, The Novel*.

S.E. INGRAHAM. Ingraham writes in Edmonton, Alberta, where she lives with the love of her life and an aging wolf/border collie. In addition to writing, she levels pictures. Her work has appeared, or will soon appear, in *Red Fez, Storm Cycle – the Best of 2012, Shot Glass, Pyrokinection, Prompted, A Handful of Stones*, and *Beyond the Dark Room*. More of her work may be found on her blog (thepoet-tree-house.blogspot.ca).

YIOTA KARIOTI. Karioti is an ancient free spirit, a fairy jester of words, and probably one of the last of her species. Her teachers in poetry include Sophocles, Seferis, Shakespeare, and Neruda. A short selection of her poems is hosted in the anthology *Fragments: Poetry, Ancient and Modern* by Blue Flute. More poetry and short stories by the Greek writer can be found on her blog, Four Seasons of My Soul (soulseasons-yiota143.blogspot.com). Follow her on Twitter as @yiota143 and on Facebook as Yiota Karioti.

MARY KLING. Wisconsin, USA. Retired Teacher. Presently Novelist, Poet, Grandmother, Photographer, Observer of Life.

ROD E. KOK. Kok has been honing his writing skills for a relatively short period of time. Starting with a personal blog, he then ventured into short stories but really found his love in poetry. He is the husband of one wife (16 years so far) and the father of two children and is proudly Canadian. He has no pets, a few hobbies, and many thoughts to turn into poems. He can be found sharing opinions on Twitter (@fifafan1969).

LAURIE KOLP. Living in Southeast Texas, Kolp is the mother of six (a husband, three kids, and two dogs). She holds a Bachelor's of Science in Curriculum and Instruction with a specialty in reading from Texas A&M University, and she is the vice-president of Texas Gulf Coast Writers. She has written poetry since she can remember and is inspired by life. You can find her on Facebook, Twitter (@KolpLaurie), her blog (lkharris-kolp.blogspot.com), and her website (lkkolp.wordpress.com).

ANDREW KREIDER. Born and raised in London, England, Kreider has lived for over twenty years in northern Indiana. He has published three chapbooks and has an active poetry blog under the title Penguin Poems (thepenguinpoet.com).

CHRIS LAWRENCE. Born in the summer of '64, Lawrence has written poetry for a number of years. He lives in West Kirby, a seaside town in the Northwest of England, with his muse and children. His work has been in a number of magazines and anthologies and has won a couple of awards.

EWAN LAWRIE. Lawrie used to do something secret in the military. Now he writes, so he's still making things up. There are bits and pieces of his work in various anthologies, and he won a prize once for a poem a while ago. There is a finished novel that no one wants. There is poetry on dVerse and some short stories, a little imagination and enough talent to put under your little fingernail. He has traveled extensively in the USA and spent considerable time in bars from Georgetown to Whidbey Island. His work is included in the following anthologies: *ABCtales Poetry Anthology*, *Voices from the Web 2012*, and *And Again Last Night*. Ewan has said that he'd like "Not everyone's cup of tea" on his headstone.

KELLY LETKY. From Farmington, New York, Letky works as a freelance graphic artist and jewelry designer. In addition to those two, she also wears the hats of photographer, writer, wife, mother, sister, daughter, crazy cat lady, friend, runner, knitter, and gardener. She writes online, sharing poetry and prose (mrsmediocrity.com) and musings about life and design (thebluemuse.com).

TONY MAUDE. Tony Maude lives near Edinburgh, Scotland. Having worked as a research chemist and then as a pastor, he now tries to make his living as a freelance proofreader. His interest in poetry resurfaced about 2 years ago when, in a difficult time in his life, poems began appearing in his head, demanding to be written down. Since then he has set about improving his awareness of poetry by reading widely and learning things they did not teach him about poetry at school. Tony is a member of the dVerse Poetry Pub team and blogs at Rumours of Rhyme (rumoursofrhyme.wordpress.com).

LORI MCCLURE. McClure, living in Cleveland, Tennessee, believes that poetry is life lived in all its juicy good and decrepit bad. Without it, our stories would sit on soul shelves waiting to be found. She has been scribbling words on paper since she was a shy little girl. Words still come, and she searches for scraps of paper to capture them before they leave. Poetry is her chosen avenue of expression. Inspiration is everywhere, in everyone, in every moment. All that's left is to pay attention.

BRIAN MILLER. Hailing from the Eastern United States, Brian Miller (waystationone.com) is a father, teacher, poet, and co-founder of dVerse Poets and One Stop Poetry.

CHARLES DAVID MILLER. A poet from Duluth, Minnesota.

DELAINA J. MILLER. A poet, librarian, and student of the world, Delaina Miller currently resides in the Midwest with her partner. Delaina enjoys teasing the soul and spirit out of everyday experiences and social injustices. Her hobbies include photography, mystery novels, and glasses of good red wine. In nice weather, she writes in the backyard, watching the birds.

ND MITCHELL. A Scottish writer who, by day, works as a high school English teacher, Mitchell shares his work at The ND's Nigh (nd-mitchell.blogspot.com). As well as poetry, he is also a writer of short stories, non-fiction, and songs (sciencekings.bandcamp.com). He loves grappling with the multi-layered meanings that poetry can accommodate as well as enjoying the adrenaline rush of understanding someone's thoughts in just a matter of a few lines. His many inspirations include Iain Crichton Smith, Edwin Morgan, Steve Turner, Robert Frost, and Sylvia Plath.

MITISURSUS. A poet from Denver, Colorado.

BEN MOELLER-GAA. A haiku poet and playwright who received a degree in creative writing from Knox College, Moeller-Gaa (benmoellergaa.com) has published poems in several journals and anthologies located in five countries on four continents and in two languages. He is a contributing editor to *River Styx* literary magazine, a member of The Haiku Foundation as well as the Haiku Society of America, and has two forthcoming haiku chapbooks, *Wasp Shadows*, published by Folded Word, and *Blowing on a Hot Soup Spoon*, published by JK Publishing's St. Louis Projects. Ben currently works for Sigma-Aldrich Corp, is a workshop leader for Studio STL, and can be seen in Wicked Pixel feature films. He lives in and travels from St. Louis, Missouri, with his wife Jessica and fluffy white cat Flitwick.

R.H. MUSTARD. Mustard has worked as a college English instructor, professional photographer, and technical rep for a large corporation, a job from which he retired in 2008. He has always written poems and has one collection, *Blue Moon*, currently available as an eBook. A second collection, *Promises*, will be out in the summer of 2013. New poems appear weekly on his blog City Noir (rhmustard.com). He and his wife Deborah live in Los Angeles.

JEFF (NICO) NEWPORT. Living in Savannah, Georgia, with his lovely wife and their lively tribe of kids, Newport finally finished his B.A. in English/Creative Writing in 2010, after wasting too many years to reckon. He appreciates poetry of all kinds, but his own work has been mostly influenced by writers such as Wendell Berry, William Wordsworth, Ted Kooser, Seamus Heaney, Jane Kenyon, and Mary Oliver. Newport invites readers to stop by his blog and visit a while (justfiddlefartingaround.blogspot.com).

ninotaziz. A Malaysian poet, an author, and storyteller of many generations born in Hobart, Tasmania, Australia, ninotaziz grew up in the idyllic village of Chenor, Malaysia, and furthered her education in Canada. Specializing in Malaysian legends, she has four anthologies of Malay and Asian legends and one novel published. Her latest novel, *Onangkiu*, was a recipient of the Calistro Award (Malaysia) in 2012. Married to Rudy Daud, she and her husband have five daughters. ninotaziz loves classic Malay hikayat and pantun, gamelan, and theatre.

ROSEMARY NISSEN-WADE. A widely-published Australian performance poet who has taught creative writing in venues from tertiary institutions to prisons, and currently a regional Neighbourhood Centre, Nissen-Wade has most recently published the book *Secret Leopard: New and Selected Poems 1974–2005* (Alyscamps Press), which is available from Amazon and from the author's website (nissen-wade.com). Nowadays her work more often appears in online magazines and anthologies than on paper, and she blogs in poetry and prose. She co-administers several poetry groups on Facebook and produces the weekly 'I Wish I'd Written This' for the online community Poets United.

POLONA OBLAK. Living and working in Ljubljana, Slovenia, Oblak discovered haiku in her early 40s and was immediately drawn to it for its concision and power of expression. Her work has appeared worldwide in various publications.

MARIO BRIAN O'CLERY. From rural County Derry, Ireland, O'Clery has been writing plays, short stories, and novels since the age of 10 and is having his first full anthology of poetry published later this year. He is also the editor in chief of the poetry blog itsapoeticalworld (itsapoeticalworld.com), which showcases original writing from members of the political discussion forum politicalworld.org. Much of his work tackles 'The Troubles' in the north of Ireland and deals with specific experiences of violent events and the outworking of growing up in such a damaged society. And trees.

WALE OWOADE. A poet and playwright born in Ogun State, Nigeria, where he also had his early education, Owoade currently lives in Ilorin, Nigeria, where he is studying history and works as a writer. Thanks to his interest in African youth literary development, he founded ARTBEAT POETRY AFRIKA (a society for African newbreed poets).

ANDRE PACE. The artistic statement to Pace's work is a "retrospective reinforced" by the remains of the verbal images... in identifying these elements they are seen afresh; it's a matter of trying to create consistent calm, perhaps even a meditative mood which would suit a number of his works / expert in petied colors with expanded expression of personality "it's not gender and identity" confront the complicated issues of conversation the text still matters! Things that seems like chance, details actually have a lot of meaning, leaving visible traces of contemporary art or modern art.

J.S. PETRI. From Bonn, Germany, Petri studies Asian languages (Tibetan, Chinese, Japanese). The poets who have inspired Petri include Novalis, Baudelaire, Rimbaud, and T.S. Eliot, among others.

SANDI PRAY. A retired high school media specialist living in the wilds of North Carolina mountains and forest marshes of North Florida, Pray is inspired by the haiku masters and a Twitter 'Band of Poets.' She began writing haiku two years ago.

SHWETANK RANA. Rana is a sailor from Himachal Pradesh, India.

UMESH RAO N. A software professional from Bangalore, India, Rao N. is fascinated with rich wordplay, imagery, metaphors, and the ability to purely express thoughts and feelings in poetry. He is inspired by Edgar Allan Poe, Dr. Seuss, and William Shakespeare and writes a blog (worthlesswordsforever.blogspot.in).

SUZY RIGG. Published poet and author, Rigg is a writer for life. Her grandfather quoted Shakespeare into his nineties. Born to Jamaican parents, the only child to a professional, glamorous mother, Rigg lived in her imagination (still does). As a corporate marketer, she writes professionally, but it's personal experiences in early childhood, turbulent adult relationships, life as a single mother, and a deep spiritual core that inspire her. A firm believer in the healing power of words, Rigg sees her work as being as much inspiration as application. Her wish is to create poems that are accessible – that make you think, smile, feel, and make your heart beat to an unheard drum. Her blog is located at theyummybone.blogspot.co.uk.

JOAN BARRETT ROBERTS. A beginning author, writer, and artist, Roberts (@jrobertswi) loves to capture ordinary moments and reflect upon the natural world and its intersection with daily life. Her professional work has been in the field of education as a public school teacher, administrator, and college professor. She also works on issues of poverty and its impact on education. In 2006, Roberts co-founded the Shadowleaves Company (facebook.com/shadowleavs) and started her blog (shadowleaves-joanie.blogspot.com). Her mission is to share the joy of writing, photography, music, and art with all ages by connecting with others. She has recently retired and lives in the beautiful Ozarks on Lake Ann in Bella Vista, Arkansas.

POLLY ROBINSON. From England, Polly is a member of Worcester Writers' Circle, Worcestershire Literary Festival, and 42 Worcester. Polly's writing has been published in many anthologies, and her first collection of poetry, *Girl's Got Rhythm*, was published in 2012. She was thrilled to be featured in the first edition of *Nain Rouge* as the result of a dVerse competition. A freelance writer and specialist educationalist, she enjoys design work and creates engaging and student-focused program material. Polly writes a blog (journalread.wordpress.com), which she started in 2011.

ROSLYN ROSS. Now living in Lilongwe, Malawi, Ross is originally from South Australia. She has worked as a journalist and editor and writes poetry, novels, non-fiction, and blogs. She also paints. What she loves about poetry is that it is painting with words. The poets who inspire her are any and all, but favorites are Shakespeare, Emily Dickinson, and Gerald Manley Hopkins. She has a strong leaning toward anything with rhyme and rhythm.

CLAUDIA SCHOENFELD. A forty-something chalk-heart drawer who (with an apron 'round her hips, lots of sugar, and a wooden cooking spoon) bakes little snapshots of her life into poetry (just to pull them out again on cooler days), Claudia lives in a small town in Germany, loves Indian food and traveling & thinks the taste of rain is just the same, no matter really where you are in the world.

DOM SCHWAB. A recent Chicago transplant, Schwab was attracted to poetry in high school, but did not become serious about it until he had graduated from college. Some poets that inspire dom: Sappho, Walt Whitman, Allen Ginsberg, Billy Collins, Tao Lin, Brandon Scott Gorrell, Ellen Kennedy, Megan Boyle, and Mira Gonzalez. His handle for both Blogger and Tumblr is "anxiouslollygagging," and his Twitter is @domschwab.

MARTIN SHONE. Living in Tettenhall, Wolverhampton, England, Shone works full-time as a school cleaner. He can't say what drew him to poetry or even who he admires or who inspires him, mainly because he forgets. "I know that I can't read some poems as they confuse the heck out of me, and I'm not a poet myself; I don't worry them till they're just so... I simply sit and write and there you have it! Poetry is a pain!"

STEVE SHULTZ. A poet and journalist from Aurora, Colorado, Shultz released his debut poetry book, *FM Ghost*, in paperback in April 2013. Read more of his writing on his blog (fmghost.wordpress.com).

VICTORIA SLOTTO. Victoria spent many years working as an RN in the field of death and dying. In retirement, she has chosen to pursue the creative life as a novelist and poet. Her first novel, *Winter is Past*, was published by Lucky Bat Books in 2011. A second, *The Sin of His Father*, and a book of poetry will be forthcoming in the near future. Victoria enjoys life with her husband and two dogs in Reno, Nevada, and Palm Desert, California. She savors the work of Mary Oliver, Stanley Kunitz, and so many others... including those in the dVerse community. She is happy to pen a monthly article for dVerse's Meeting the Bar that deals with the art and craft of poetry writing.

KELVIN S.M. A self-proclaimed poet, a former stage actor, a crayon-artist, a mythical sleuth, a Filipino (with a small mix of Spanish blood), and a chess enthusiast, Kelvin finished college in 2011 and currently works as a corporate accountant in a real estate company in the Philippines. He started writing poems at age 15, when he was introduced to haiku and sonnets by the Brownings and Shakespeare.

SHANE STANISAUSKIS. Twenty-eight years old, from Greater Manchester, Great Britain, Stanisauskis works in the care system with young people as a residential support worker. He is also a rapper/poet and a member of the "liberation squad" movement. He first got into poetry at eleven years old when seeing a psychiatrist, who suggested writing his feelings down. Naturally he noticed words rhyming, and that was it!

GEETA SURI. "Words when tugs my heart, swirls my nerves and spins my head, I give them the way out through my pen." Suri loves to learn and try new things. Indian by heart, mind, and soul, the creative bug bit her when she was in school. She used to paint a canvas with colors as well as with words. Words of appreciation started showering upon her, and that was something more inspiring. The first person who pushed her towards writing was her mother, and she still encourages her constantly. She has been her best critic ever. Suri pens online as Odyzz (Odizzey.wordpress.com).

MART STEL. From the Netherlands, Stel makes and publishes "haikuphotos" under the name of MartsArts. The project began in 2013, mostly inspired by the processes within and between people. Therefore, they are in fact more "senryu" than "haiku." Stel publishes this work on Twitter (@martsarts) and on his blog (martsart.wordpress.com).

TOM SWANSTON. From Woking, Surrey, UK, Swanston is a screenwriter and film producer. Having studied anthropology at Durham University, he went on to produce feature films and shorts, winning awards in Cannes and New York. He is currently producing a comedy feature about the collapse of a bank. His other interests include portraiture, golf, powerlifting, and dancing. He loves writing comic poetry and takes inspiration from Roald Dahl and Carol-Ann Duffy.

VAL TERMANE. Born September 3, 1979, Termane is a Portuguese poet who writes both in Portuguese and in English. He has written *Amanhã Chovi* (2012) and *Pelagus* (2013) in his mother-tongue under the pen name Alexandre Homem Dual. Inspired by poets such as Fernando Pessoa, Camilo Pessanha, and Herberto Helder – or Walt Whitman, Edgar Allan Poe, and Charles Bukowski – his writings dwell between a pessimistic vitalism and a vitalist pessimism. He is also the author of two literary blogs, Amendual (amendual.blogspot.com, in Portuguese) and One Poem and A Few Lullabies (onepoemandafewlullabies.tumblr.com).

DIANNE TURNER. Turner lives at Godwin Beach in Queensland, Australia, a most beautiful part of the world. She has been writing poetry since she was a teenager. Writing has been a part of her life from early school years. Australian poets Judith Wright, Bruce Dawe, Gloria B Yates, and Dorothy Hewett have all been inspirations, and she does love the Beats too, particularly Jack Kerouac and Frank O'Hara. Her favorite poem is Frank O'Hara's "Why I Am Not a Painter." Firstly Dianne is a mother, but has been a teacher aide, business owner, and is now pursuing art and writing. Whatever she does in life, it seems she always returns to both art and writing, which she considers to be a part of her. You can see both of her creative forms at her blog (pandamoniumcat.wordpress.com).

LILY WANG. A poet from Hangzhou, China, Wang shares her work on her blog (lilybyanyothername.wordpress.com).

JENNIFER WAGNER. A poet who writes at www.poetlaundry.com and lives in the Pacific Northwest with her firefighter husband and their four amazing sons.

R.E. WARNER. An independent writer locked in a desperate search for novelty. As easily amused as he is bored, Warner persistently dumps work on the World Wide Web at Troped.com in the hopes that someone will notice. After all, novelty should be a two-way street.

FRANK WATSON. Editor of this volume, Watson was born in Venice, California and now lives in New York City. He enjoys literature, art, calligraphy, history, jazz, and all aspects of international culture and travel. His previous books include *Fragments: poetry, ancient & modern* (editor) and *One Hundred Leaves: a new, annotated translation of the Hyakunin Isshu* (editor and translator). His work has appeared in *Rosebud* and *Bora* literary magazines. Frank shares his work on his Twitter account (@FollowBlueFlute) and on his blog (www.followtheblueflute.com).

MARVIN WELBORN. Writer and poet, Welborn lives in retirement from the global financial markets and writes fulltime in Charlottesville, Virginia, among the lovely foothills of the magnificent Blue Ridge Mountains, betwixt the homes of Thomas Jefferson and James Madison, and more often than not between the Sun and the Moon.

MARIA WELLMAN. Wellman is a poet from Butler, Pennsylvania.

CHRISTENA WILLIAMS. A Jamaican poet, Williams has been featured 29 times in The Gleaner newspaper of Jamaica, poetry anthologies, and magazines. She loves old classic souls and Bob Marley. In her leisure time she writes rap lyrics, poetry, text; surfs the net; reads books; and watches Law and Order SVU, CSI, Bones, Castle, and beIN Sport. She loves adventure and mystery books. She sees herself as a radical poet and aspires to become a criminal lawyer. She is inspired by Maya Angelou, Louise Bennett, and songs from Bob Marley as well as Think Out Loud poets. Drawn to poetry during times of pain, she reads Maya Angelou, who speaks through her ink.

MARK WINDHAM. Living in the suburbs of Atlanta, GA with his wife and two of his children (and three dogs), Windham is an entrepreneur and a recently awakened writer. Some of his work has appeared in *The Dead Mule Society for Southern Literature*, *The River Journal*, and *Postcard Shorts*, among others.

TIARA WINTER-SCHORR. A New York City writer and a regular contributor to *Numero Cinq Magazine*, Winter-Schorr has a B.A. in Creative Writing from Columbia University. She is drawn to poetry because poems are the rawest form of self-expression. Pablo Neruda, Walt Whitman, Anne Sexton, and Jorie Graham have always been sources of inspiration and influence for her.

www.ingramcontent.com/pod-product-compliance
Lightning Source LLC
Chambersburg PA
CBHW021923040426
42448CB00008B/887